In *Rejoice!* Chris Wright expl i
throughout the Scriptures tc t
Christmas, and to raise our
at the climax of history. Wh
simply some lessons from the .
that our lives only really make
this book and have your mind expanded and your heart warmed.
Read it and rejoice!
Tim Chester, Pastor, Grace Church, Boroughbridge, North
Yorkshire, and a faculty member of Crosslands Training

Written with deceptive simplicity, these devotions show the heart-
rendingly beautiful character of a God who comes to his children
again and again and again. They show that Advent is not just for
Christmas, but from before time and beyond it. These readings will
draw you deeper into the Bible's big story so that your heart rejoices
in a good God who comes to us and draws us close so that we can
enjoy him for ever.
Mark Ellis, Director of CU Ireland

REJOICE!

All the royalties from this book have been irrevocably assigned to Langham Literature. Langham Literature is a ministry of Langham Partnership, founded by John Stott. Chris Wright is the International Ministries Director.

Langham Literature provides Majority World preachers, scholars and seminary libraries with evangelical books and electronic resources through publishing and distribution, grants and discounts. They also foster the creation of indigenous evangelical books in many languages through writers' grants, strengthening local evangelical publishing houses and investment in major regional literature projects.

For further information on Langham Literature, and the rest of Langham Partnership, visit the website at <www.langham.org>.

REJOICE!

Advent in all the Scriptures

Chris Wright
with
John Stott

INTER-VARSITY PRESS
36 Causton Street, London SW1P 4ST, England
Email: ivp@ivpbooks.com
Website: www.ivpbooks.com

© Chris Wright, 2019

Chris Wright has asserted his right under the Copyright, Designs and Patents Act 1988
to be identified as Author of this work.

All rights reserved. No part of this publication may be reproduced, stored
in a retrieval system, or transmitted, in any form or by any means, electronic,
mechanical, photocopying, recording or otherwise, without the prior permission
of the publisher or the Copyright Licensing Agency.

Unless otherwise indicated, Scripture quotations are taken from the Holy Bible, New
International Version (Anglicized edition). Copyright © 1979, 1984, 2011 by Biblica.
Used by permission of Hodder & Stoughton Ltd, an Hachette UK company. All rights
reserved. 'NIV' is a registered trademark of Biblica. UK trademark number 1448790.

Scripture quotations marked ESV are taken from the ESV® Bible (The Holy Bible, English
Standard Version®) copyright © 2001 by Crossway, a publishing ministry of Good News
Publishers. ESV® Text Edition: 2011. The ESV® text has been reproduced in cooperation
with and by permission of Good News Publishers. Unauthorized reproduction
of this publication is prohibited. All rights reserved.

Extracts marked KJV are from the Authorized Version of the Bible (The King James
Bible), the rights in which are vested in the Crown, and are reproduced by permission
of the Crown's Patentee, Cambridge University Press.

The Scripture quotation marked MSG is from THE MESSAGE. Copyright © 1993, 1994,
1995, 1996, 2000, 2001, 2002. Used by permission of NavPress Publishing Group.

All emphases in Scripture quotations have been added by the author.

First published 2019

British Library Cataloguing-in-Publication Data
A catalogue record for this book is available from the British Library.

ISBN: 978–1–78359–936–3
eBook ISBN: 978–1–78359–937–0

Set in 11/14 pt Minion Pro
Typeset in Great Britain by CRB Associates, Potterhanworth, Lincolnshire
Printed in Great Britain by Ashford Colour Press Ltd, Gosport, Hampshire

*Inter-Varsity Press publishes Christian books that are true to the Bible and that
communicate the gospel, develop discipleship and strengthen the church for its mission
in the world.*

*IVP originated within the Inter-Varsity Fellowship, now the Universities and Colleges
Christian Fellowship, a student movement connecting Christian Unions in universities
and colleges throughout Great Britain, and a member movement of the International
Fellowship of Evangelical Students. Website: www.uccf.org.uk. That historic association
is maintained, and all senior IVP staff and committee members subscribe to the
UCCF Basis of Faith.*

Contents

List of abbreviations   x

Preface   xiii

Introduction   1

Week 1
THE GOD WHO COMES IN SCRIPTURE'S STORY

1 God comes rejoicing in creation (act 1)   7
   Psalm 104

2 God comes questioning sinners (act 2)   11
   Genesis 3

3 God comes with a promise (act 3)   15
   Genesis 18:1–21

4 God comes bringing light and life (act 4)   19
   John 1:1–14

5 God comes sending us to the nations (act 5)   23
   Luke 24:36–53; Acts 1:1–11

6 God comes to put things right (act 6)   27
   Matthew 25:31–46; John 5:24–29

7 God comes creating a whole new world (act 7)   31
   Isaiah 60

Week 2
THE GOD WHO CAME IN PERSON

8 My Rock and my salvation   37
   Psalm 62

Contents

9   God comes to the rescue   41
    Exodus 2:23 – 3:10

10 God comes to speak   45
    Exodus 19:1–9, 16–19; 20:18–21

11 God comes for a meal   49
    Exodus 24:1–11

12 God comes to stay   53
    Exodus 25:1–8; 29:42–46

13 God comes to forgive   57
    Exodus 32:1–14; 33:18 – 34:9

14 God comes to lead the way   61
    Exodus 40:17–38

Week 3
THE GOD WHO CAME AS PROMISED

15 Waiting for God   67
    Psalm 40

16 Running with good news   70
    Isaiah 52:7–10

17 A Ruler from Bethlehem – of all places!   74
    Micah 5:1–5

18 God is on his way! Get ready and repent   78
    Luke 1:57–80

19 Are you the One who is to come?   82
    Matthew 11:2–6; Isaiah 35

20 Light for the nations   86
    Luke 2:22–35

21 The sin-bearing Servant   90
    Isaiah 52:13 – 53:12

Contents

Week 4
THE GOD WHO WILL COME IN GLORY

22 Creation rejoices   97
    Psalm 96

23 Creation renewed   101
    Isaiah 65:17–25; 2 Peter 3:3–13

24 Creation redeemed   105
    Romans 8:16–25

25 Immanuel: God with us!   109
    Revelation 21:1–5

Abbreviations

BC	*Basic Christianity* (IVP, 2008)
BISTY	*But I Say to You* (IVP 2013): updated version of *Christ the Controversialist*
BST	The Bible Speaks Today (IVP series, normally followed by name of Bible book): *Acts* (IVP, 1991); *Romans* (IVP, 1994); *Ephesians* (IVP, 1991); *Thessalonians* (IVP, 1991)
CMMW	*Christian Mission in the Modern World* (IVP, 2016)
ET	*Evangelical Truth* (IVP, 2015)
FP	*Favourite Psalms* (Candle Books, 1994)
IFCT	*Issues Facing Christians Today* (Zondervan, 2006)
IS	*Inside Story* by Roger Steer (IVP, 2009)
JS: APBHF	*John Stott: A Portrait by His Friends*, edited by Christopher J. H. Wright (IVP, 2011)
JS: TMOAL	*John Stott: The Making of a Leader* by Timothy Dudley-Smith (IVP, 2012)
LCOWE	Lausanne Congress on World Evangelism
LP	Langham Partnership
TBOT	*The Birds Our Teachers* (Candle Books, 1999)
TBTY	*Through the Bible through the Year* (Candle Books, 2006)
TCC	The Contemporary Christian series, consisting of five books: *The Gospel* (TG; IVP, 2019), *The Disciple* (TD; IVP, 2019), *The Bible* (TB; IVP, 2019), *The Church* (TC; IVP, 2019), *The World* (TW; IVP, 2019) (formerly published as one volume: *The Contemporary Christian*, 1992)
TCOC	*The Cross of Christ* (IVP, 2006)
TIC	*The Incomparable Christ* (IVP, 2014)

List of abbreviations

TLC	*The Living Church* (IVP, 2014)
TRD	*The Radical Disciple* (IVP, 2013)
WIAAC	*Why I Am a Christian* (IVP, 2013)

Preface

It has long seemed to me that Advent is something of a Cinderella in the church's year – rather overlooked and sometimes downright ill-treated. We all love the Christmas season, Easter is a joyful celebration, and there are those who take Lent quite seriously as a time of self-denial in some way. But Advent? Like people who were careless enough to be born near the end of December and find that nobody can remember their birthday, let alone celebrate it, the weeks of Advent are simply buried under the avalanche of approaching Christmas.

Liturgically minded churches will say the Advent Collect on Advent Sunday, but may forget to include it the following weeks (though it is a beautiful, biblical and challenging prayer, well worth repeating). We might get to sing 'O Come, O Come, Emmanuel', but so drearily that it seems weirdly out of tune with the bells and angels of carol services and nativity plays. And being told that Advent is all about the *second coming* can also be heard as a bit of a dampener on the festive season, when it's often hard enough to tell the world that Christmas is about Christ's *first coming*.

And what should an Advent devotional book do? Well, there are many fine examples of the genre, of course, and most of them take the reader through nourishing reflections on some part of the Bible, but not always with direct relevance to the prime theme of Advent itself – that the Lord our God is the God who comes! And yet the Bible is full, literally from beginning to end, with accounts of God coming in all kinds of ways and with all kinds of results. These range from the distant past to the guaranteed future, from creation to new creation.

There is an acclamation in the Anglican service of Holy Communion, which joyfully affirms, 'Christ has died. Christ is risen. Christ will come again.' Perhaps the motto for this book could be: 'God has come. God keeps coming. God will come again.' My hope is that this short book will be a source of daily rejoicing as you trace the comings of God in all the Scriptures.

I would like to thank Eleanor Trotter of IVP, who invited me to write this book, suggested the idea of combining my own reflections with short quotations from or about John Stott (to whom we owe so much in our love for the Bible and our motivation to understand and rejoice in all that God has revealed to us in it), and has helped to shape and edit the text with great care.

Chris Wright

Introduction
The God who comes and comes –
and comes again

Welcome to a book that I hope will give you daily reasons to rejoice! Welcome right into the very heart of Advent.

What is Advent anyway? The clue is in the name. It means 'a coming'. But not just any old coming. It is *the coming of God*. And so, as a season of the church's year, it fits nicely into the weeks before Christmas as we celebrate God's coming in a manger in Bethlehem. And it invites us to prepare also for his promised coming again – Christ's 'second advent' as it gets called.

But those two advents are far from the only times God has or will come. The Bible is full of God's 'comings'. Naturally, then, an Advent book has to take us to the Bible. But what do you think the Bible actually is? For some, it is a book full of promises, precious thoughts to get us through each day. For others, it is a book full of rules, God's instructions and guidance for how to live in a way that pleases him. For others, the Bible is a book full of doctrines, teaching us the truths that God has revealed which we need to distil and understand.

Well, there are plenty of promises, rules and doctrines in the Bible, for sure. But the Bible itself, as a whole, is much more than any or all of the above.

The Bible presents itself to us, in its grand structure, as one whole story. Not just any story, but *The Story* of the universe. It has a beginning, when God created the heavens and the earth. And it has an ending, when God will bring about the renewal of all creation. And in between it tells the story of what went wrong, and what God has done in history to put things right.

1

Since this is not just a story that we observe or tell, but one in which we actively participate as actors, it can be thought of as a great Drama – the drama of Scripture – with seven acts.

Here it is in a simple diagram that fits on the back of an envelope. (I know that because I've done it there, and also on the back of restaurant napkins, when explaining the idea of the Bible as one whole story to friends.)

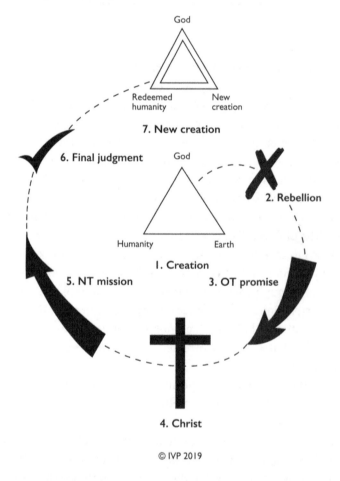

© IVP 2019

Act 1 Creation: God created the heavens and earth, and placed human beings, made in his own image, in the earth, to rule and serve there.

Act 2 *Rebellion*: We chose to disobey God's instructions, and decide for ourselves what we think is good and evil. We brought sin, death and division into human life, and brokenness into creation itself.

Act 3 *OT promise*: God promised that he would bring blessing and salvation, where we had brought curse and death. Through Abraham, he launched the people, Israel, through whom the good news of that blessing would ultimately embrace all nations on earth. The Old Testament story is constantly moving forward towards the fulfilment of that promise.

Act 4 *Christ*: The central act of the whole Bible story is what we read in the Gospels, according to the first four books of the New Testament, about Jesus of Nazareth, Messiah and Lord, in his incarnation, his life and teaching, his atoning death, his victorious resurrection and his ascension to glory and cosmic government.

Act 5 *NT mission*: the drama continues with the outpouring of the Holy Spirit and the launch of the mission of the church – comprising both believing Jews and Gentiles – to the ends of the earth.

Act 6 *Final judgment*: The good news is that evil will not have the last word, and God will ultimately put all things right (which is what judgment means in the Bible) by dealing with and destroying all that is wrong and evil. Act 6 is the completion of God's answer to act 2, and of the accomplishment of act 4.

Act 7 *New creation*: The Bible drama ends with a dramatic new beginning! After putting all things right, God will make all things new, and will come to dwell with redeemed humanity in his restored creation, for ever.

Now here's the thing. *God comes*, and comes, and comes again – all the way through this great biblical drama and in every act within it. God just keeps on coming! And that can be a matter of joy, relief, fear, comfort or hope, depending on what is going on when he comes. So this explains the subtitle of our book, *Advent in All the Scriptures*. Top tip: keep a marker in the drama with the seven acts above, to help you locate where you are in the story at any given time.

I hope you will find that these daily reflections, drawn from every part of the Bible's story – including the parts that give us hope and assurance about things that haven't yet happened – will indeed lead you on a journey of rejoicing and encouragement and deepened faith.

Week 1 (starting on 1 December)

THE GOD WHO COMES IN SCRIPTURE'S STORY

In week 1 of Advent, let's take a whistle-stop tour through the whole Bible story, selecting for each day a passage that relates to each of those seven great acts outlined in the Introduction. Let's be ready to welcome daily the God who comes in every act of the biblical drama.

A prayer for week 1 of Advent

Almighty God, give us grace to cast away the works of darkness and to put on the armour of light, now in the time of this mortal life, in which your Son Jesus Christ came to us in great humility. And so, on the last day, when he shall come again in his glorious majesty to judge the living and the dead, may we rise to the life immortal. We pray this through him who is alive and reigns with you and the Holy Spirit, one God, now and for ever. Amen.

1

God comes rejoicing in creation (act 1)

Bible reading: Psalm 104

From John Stott:

> I always keep my binoculars on my desk within easy reach of
> my right hand.
> ('The Hookses: A Writer's Retreat', JS: TMOAL, p. 439)

> The widely accepted estimate is that there are about 9,000
> different species [of birds] in the world . . . Although I have
> had the privilege of travelling in many countries and habitats,
> I have seen only about 2,500 species.
>   Only one person has seen them all, and that of course is
> God himself, their creator '. . . So God created . . . every winged
> bird according to its kind. And God saw that it was good'
> (Genesis 1:20–21). In consequence, he is able to claim: 'I know
> all the birds of the air, and the creatures of the field are mine'
> (Psalm 50:11, literally). More than that, since Jesus said that
> not a single Sparrow falls to the ground without the know-
> ledge of God (Matthew 10:29), he must know not only every
> species of bird, but every individual member of each species as
> well. And that would mean many thousands of millions.
> (TBOT, pp. 8–9)

*

We love taking our grandchildren to Zoomarine in southern
Portugal. You should see their amazed faces and sparkling eyes as

they watch the dolphins in the aquarium. What amazing tricks, leaps and somersaults those dolphins perform, as their trainers ply them with balls, ride upright on their backs, dive to the depths of the pool, and reward them with fish! Surely those are smiles on the dolphins' faces too.

And every time Psalm 104:26 comes to mind, telling me that God created the great creatures of the ocean ('Leviathan' is a symbolic term that could include whales), for God himself to play with there! One version (NIV) says, 'which you formed to frolic there'. But the Hebrew can just as clearly mean, 'which you formed *to play with*' (ESV footnote). I wonder if the idea of God splashing about doing tricks with whales and dolphins and enjoying the fun appeals to you as much as it does to me!

God comes to his creation in all kinds of ways in Psalm 104 – and with exuberant joy (verse 31). Now, of course, we have the more carefully ordered portrait of creation in Genesis 1 (where God systematically moulds creation into his own cosmic temple, complete with his image – not a statue, but living human beings – and then 'rests' there to rule and sustain the good order of heaven and earth). But this psalmist takes those great creational moments and turns them into exquisitely delightful poetic images. The singer is revelling in the sheer wonders of creation and imagines God doing the same. This is shared joy. This is rejoicing shared by God, by humans and by all living creatures, and indeed even by the inanimate creation.

God moves around his creation, like an invisible magician, 'dressed up in sunshine' (verse 2, MSG), turning the sky into a tent, the earth into a house, the winds and clouds into his transport (verses 2–5). His command governs, at one extreme, the mighty waters that once swamped mountains, turning them into harmless drinking troughs for thirsty animals, and at the other extreme, every blade of grass that grows for hungry cattle, and the humble soil that brings forth wine, oil and bread to sustain, gladden and beautify human life (verses 6–15).

God's loving provision, however, is far wider than merely what supports human life, such as our agriculture, our domestic animals and our daily work (verse 23). The psalmist also celebrates those parts of creation which (as far as he knew at that time) held no direct human benefit – high mountains, cedar forests, wild birds, little animals scurrying round the crags, and nocturnal beasts of prey (verses 16–18, 20–22). These too belong to God. They matter to God (as they should also to us, of course).

The sea! The psalmist gasps in awe as he visualizes it (verse 25), with its teeming life under the surface (and all he knew was the Mediterranean – a mere pond compared with the vast oceans). Of course, the sea provides boundless pathways for shipping (verse 26), but long before humans found it useful for commerce, God and the whales were enjoying it as their playground.

Then God comes as zookeeper and vet, feeding the animals at just the right time and from his own hand – delightfully direct and hands-on (verses 27–28). Of course, animals die and give birth and life is renewed, and God's Spirit is at work in that great cycle of life just as he was in the first act of creation (verses 29–30; Genesis 1:2).

To all God's creation, then, *God comes*: ordering, establishing, regulating, supplying, enjoying, and supremely and fearfully governing (verse 32). And the psalmist is simply lost in wonder, love and praise at the glory of God revealed in the superabundant plenitude of all God's creatures and works (verses 1, 24, 33).

Follow the psalmist's example today. Take time to marvel at the works of God's hands, and give thanks. Advent is a great time to recover the joy of God coming to us in and through his spectacular creation – right down to the food and drink on our breakfast table and all that has contributed to it being there.

So is the last prayer of the psalmist out of place then?

> But may sinners vanish from the earth
>   and the wicked be no more.
> (verse 35)

Frankly, it jars on us, after the joy of the rest of the psalm. But no, it is not out of place. For God's good creation also suffers in broken-ness and frustration because of human sin, and the psalmist knows this and longs for God to deal with it. Though, of course, if God were to answer his prayer literally for a moment, not one of us would be left on the planet. God had a better plan – for sinners and for creation, as we shall see on this Advent journey together.

A prayer
God comes when God sends his Spirit (verse 30), as we know from God's Son Jesus himself, for ourselves and for the church.

Pray that this Advent you may experience the life-giving and re-newing power of the Spirit, the same Spirit that renews the life of the earth and all God's creatures.

2

God comes questioning sinners (act 2)

Bible reading: Genesis 3

From John Stott:

> Between the ideal and the reality there was a great gulf fixed.
> I had high ideals but a weak will.
> (JS: TMOAL, p. 89)

> Not just is our fallen nature crookedly bent, twisted, self-
> absorbed and self-obsessed. We have risen up in active
> rebellion against a holy God. We have certainly not loved him
> with all our being . . . When sin is stripped of all its disguises,
> and is seen in its ugly nakedness as the attempt to dethrone
> God and enthrone self, it is evident that we are incapable of
> doing anything to gain acceptance with God.
> (ET, p. 53)

*

'If God's got the whole world in his hands, what's he standing on?'
asked our four-year-old grandson in all seriousness and some
literal-minded anxiety.

Children ask the most challenging questions that get right down
to cosmic truths and mysteries, like how the God whom we can't
see is powerful enough to hold up the earth (without standing on
anything!).

The first question in the Bible comes from a serpent, throwing
suspicion on God's truthfulness. 'Did God really say . . . ?' (verse 1).

The next question, and questions, come from God, addressed to the first humans, but ringing in our own ears ever since: 'Where are you?' (verse 9) and 'What have you done?' (verse 13). And in between the serpent's question and God's comes the story often referred to as the 'fall', though that's hardly an adequate term for what happened. We didn't just *fall* into sin, like we accidentally tripped up. *We chose to rebel*, distrusted God's goodness, disregarded God's warning, disobeyed his instructions. And the rest, as they say, is history – horrible history, bristling with evil, brutality and greed, wet with tears and suffering, slashed with all the scars inflicted by act 2 of the great drama of Scripture (see diagram on p. 2).

What Genesis 3 portrays is not 'the origin of evil' – the Bible never explains that. Rather, it describes the *entrance* of evil and sin into *human* experience. For we chose to collude with some evil source that was not God. We gave in to the temptation to decide for ourselves what is good and evil, rather than trusting God to be the judge of that. We chose the path of moral autonomy. Made in the image of God in order to be like him, we wanted more – to be *as* God, to be our own god. And so the idolatry of the self (the seed of all other idolatries) takes root in the welcoming soil of the human heart.

In a very simple way, but with profound insight, the story shows how every dimension of the human person was involved in the first act of human disobedience.

Spiritually, the Woman has given in to the serpent's sneering at God's motives and denial of God's judgment – alienation from God is already in motion. *Mentally*, she exercises the good gifts of God to humankind: rational evaluation of a good food source, aesthetic appreciation of beauty, and a desire for wisdom. Nothing wrong with those thoughts in themselves – except that these wonderful human abilities are now being used to justify a course of action that God had clearly forbidden. *Physically*, she takes bodily action in the created world in an act of direct disobedience. 'She took . . . and ate: so simple the act, but so hard its undoing. God will taste poverty and death before "take and eat" become verbs of salvation.'[1] And *relationally*, she shared it with her husband 'who was with her' (please note, gentlemen), and so the sin that had invaded the spiritual, intellectual and physical realms of human existence corrupted our social relationships also.

Two effects were immediate, and have remained characteristic of fallen human life ever since: shame in the presence of one another (verse 7) and fear in the presence of God (verse 10). At least, they *should* characterize us, but as Paul observes in Romans 1, we reach an advanced stage of depravity when we can sin *without* shame or the fear of God.

A third effect in the story is something we have honed to perfection: the skill of blaming anybody else but ourselves (verses 12–13). The story wends its gloomy way through Genesis 4 – 11. Sin escalates into jealousy, anger and murder within families, and full-blown corruption and violence in society. Sin multiplies through successive generations of history, brings division and confusion to the world of nations and cultures, and affects the whole created order.

Why such morbid reflections so early in Advent? Because, unless we take seriously the Bible's radical diagnosis of the human predicament, we will not understand the need for the rest of the Bible's story of redemption. Advent, of course, brings us good news. It is a season of gospel joy and a crescendo of hope. But that good news is so good precisely because the bad news is so bad. And today we remember why. It is into *this* world that God brings hope and joy.

Already good news is glimmering through Genesis 3, though. God promises that evil will not have the last word: a human descendant of Eve will crush the serpent's head (verse 15). God provides more durable clothing, as an act of mercy and grace even to the disobedient (verse 21). And God prevents us from grasping immortality also in our sinful and rebellious state (verses 22–24). God has better plans and a better way for us to gain eternal life – though at a cost known only to himself.

---

1 Derek Kidner, *Genesis: An Introduction and Commentary*, Tyndale Old Testament Commentaries (IVP, 1967), p. 68.

A reflection

Still today God comes questioning sinners – and saints, for we are both. How will you answer him today?

- 'Where are you?' Here we are, we respond, enjoying God's creation gifts, yet suffering also in creation's brokenness. We are creatures of acts 1 and 2 of the Bible drama.
- 'What have you done?' Here we are, we respond, sinners like Adam and Eve and needing to repent daily. Yet here we are also as God's redeemed children. God asks, 'What have you done, what will you do today, that flows from faith, love and gratitude for God's saving grace in the gospel of Christ?'

3

God comes with a promise (act 3)

Bible reading: Genesis 18:1–21

From John Stott:

> He bore the curse in order that we might inherit the blessing promised to Abraham.
> (TCOC, p. 175)

> It is no exaggeration to say that Genesis 12:1–4 is the most unifying text of the whole Bible. For God's saving purpose to bless the whole world through Christ, who was Abraham's seed, is encapsulated here. The rest of the Bible is an unfolding of this text, and subsequent history has seen its fulfilment . . . We ourselves would not be followers of Jesus today if it were not for this text: we are beneficiaries of the promise God made to Abraham . . . (Gal. 3:26–29).
> (TW, TCC series, p. 40)

*

With act 3 of the biblical drama, we embark on a very long journey indeed – the whole of the rest of the Old Testament. And it all begins with a meal in the afternoon outside a tent. Well, almost. It actually began twenty-four years and six chapters earlier, in Genesis 12, but not a lot has happened in the meantime (though Hagar might disagree) – and that's exactly the problem.

When you've read through Genesis 3 – 11, you might wonder, 'What can God do next? Does he have any answer to the escalating wickedness, violence and arrogance of humankind?' We turn to Genesis 12 and we find that, yes, indeed God does, though I can imagine a sharp intake of breath among the incredulous angels when he unveiled it. God loves surprises (as Gabriel will find out). So God points to a Middle Eastern migrant called Abram and his wife Sarai and says, 'There's my answer. Starting with that couple, I will create a nation through whom I will flood the earth and all nations upon it with my blessing – just like I did at creation.' Sounds like a plan. Well, except . . .

The only snag (as some courageous angel might have drawn to the divine attention) was that Abram was already seventy-five years old, and his wife Sarai, though ten years younger (17:17) and beautiful enough to be lied for (12:11–14), had not yet conceived a child, and was well past the age when she could. But 'Is anything too hard for the LORD?' God may have asked the angels with a smile, before putting the same question to Sarah (18:14), when he turned up for that afternoon meal.

For the problem was that years before, God had promised Abraham and Sarah (as God renamed them) a son of their own. But nothing had happened, and now they are both well past the pleasure or the possibility. *Laughable!* That's what the whole idea seemed to them both (17:17; 18:12) – which is why they named him Isaac ('The Laughing One') when he finally arrived (21:1–7).

Take a quick look at the first time God came to Abraham in Genesis 12:1–3. God told him to migrate to an unspecified destination, and he made him three big promises and one colossal one. The first three promises were: that he would have descendants who would become a great nation (the people of Israel); that there would be a relationship of covenant blessing between God and this people; and that God would give them a land to live in. Act 3 gets under way as those promises are fulfilled.

What about that colossal promise? It comes as the bottom line (Genesis 12:3): through Abraham and Sarah and their descendants, God would enable all nations on earth to participate in some way in God's blessing.

Blessing for *all* nations! That's very good news indeed in the wake of Genesis 11! So good, in fact, that Paul will quote Genesis 12:3 and call it 'the gospel in advance' (Galatians 3:8).

God's promise to Abraham keeps the goal of God's universal mission always in view in the background, even when Israel is mostly in the foreground. Act 3 of the Bible drama is always pointing forward to something beyond its own horizon – the world of all nations and the whole earth. So this is the world's story, not just Israel's.

When my two sons were young, they played for their primary school football team. I would go along with my SLR camera and a telephoto lens. With one eye looking through the lens, I could fill the whole frame close-up with one of my boys. With my other eye open, I could be aware of the rest of the players and the movement of the game. I might focus close-up on Tim, my firstborn. But Tim was only there because a match was going on with all the other players involved.

So it is in act 3 of the Bible. The focus is mostly on Israel ('my firstborn son', says God to Pharaoh; Exodus 4:22). *But Israel is only there because God has a great plan and purpose for all nations on earth to experience his redemptive blessing.* That's God's mission, God's agenda. And that's where this story is headed.

You'll find this awareness especially in Israel's prayer and worship, and in the vision of some of the prophets. You may not have time today, but come back and have a look at these texts, and hear the echoes of God's great promise to Abraham: 1 Kings 8:41–43; Psalms 22:27; 47:9; 86:9; Isaiah 49:6; Zechariah 2:11. God's dealings with Israel are for the sake of his plan for all nations.

So, when the angel Gabriel makes his surprise announcement to Zechariah and Mary at the start of act 4, both of them will rejoice that God is keeping his promise to Abraham (Luke 1:54–55, 72–73). And, as Simeon recognizes, the birth of Jesus (and his death) will be for the glory of Israel and *a light for the nations* (Luke 2:25–35).

A challenge

There's a challenge for Abraham and his people in verse 19. If they are to be the vehicle of God's blessing for the nations, then they must walk in the way of the Lord, in righteousness and justice – very different from the ways of Sodom and Gomorrah.

If we are to participate in God's mission to the nations, then, similarly, there is for us an ethical challenge to live in God's way, not the world's. There can be no biblical mission without biblical living.

4

God comes bringing light and life (act 4)

Bible reading: John 1:1–14

Always ready to share his own resources with others, he took endless trouble, never sparing himself.
(Frances Whitehead, John Stott's secretary for fifty-five years, Thanksgiving tribute)

'I am among you,' Jesus said, 'as one who serves' (Luke 22:27). So he gave himself in selfless service for others . . . he served in deed as well as in word, and it would be impossible in the ministry of Jesus to separate his works from his words. He fed hungry mouths and washed dirty feet, he healed the sick, comforted the sad and even restored the dead to life. Now he sends us, he says, as the Father had sent him.

Therefore our mission, like his, is to be one of service . . . He supplies us with the perfect model of service, and sends his church into the world to be a servant church . . . it is in our servant role that we can find the right synthesis of evangelism and social action . . . both authentic expressions of the love that serves.
(John Stott, CMMW, pp. 23–25)

*

You're watching a serialized television drama over several weeks. With each new episode, there's a short sequence of flashbacks to previous ones, to remind you of the story so far. Each flashback, only a few seconds long, flags up in your memory whole chunks of a plot that might have filled hours of viewing.

All four Gospels launch into act 4 of the great biblical drama, with many flashbacks to the Old Testament.

Can you see all the first three acts in today's Bible reading?

John begins with act 1, the uncreated Word of God calling all created things into existence (1:1–4). He then contrasts the life and light of the Word with the darkness of our fallen world (act 2), a world that neither recognized nor received him when he came into it (1:4–5, 9–11). And then he portrays how the Word became flesh and 'tabernacled' among us (1:14) – an allusion to the way God came to dwell among Israel at Mount Sinai in act 3. And now, in act 4, the grace and truth that had been revealed to Israel through Moses have now 'come' – embodied and multiplied in Jesus Christ – 'grace in place of grace already given', as John puts it (1:16–17).

In act 4 of the Bible drama, then, the God we know from acts 1 and 3 (see diagram on p. 2) enters the world in person to deal with the consequences unleashed by act 2. *God comes.* God the *Creator* of the world, God the *Redeemer* of Israel, *this God* comes to us in Word made flesh. John 1:14 is Advent in a nutshell. Advent gospel. Advent rejoicing!

John's Gospel plays Advent music throughout, for Jesus talks often about how and why he had come. Spend a moment of grateful reflection on each of the four groups of texts below. (Read one text in each group now and come back later for a second helping.)

Jesus came as light in the darkness (3:16–21; 8:12–14). Echoing his prologue (1:5), John says that when God sent his Son into this sinful world, it was as the arrival of light into darkness. Jesus came *into* darkness so that we can come *out of* darkness. From death to life is God's invitation. Or go on hiding in the darkness of evil deeds and lies. That is the stark choice we face.

Jesus came with his Father's authority (5:37–43; 7:16–17, 27–29). The first advent of Jesus was surrounded by controversy. Religious leaders sneered. Ordinary people were confused. Where had he come from? What right did he have to say such outrageous things? Jesus' answer was very clear. He had come because he had been sent by his Father. All he did and said was in his Father's name. It was as though God the Father himself were present, acting and speaking through Jesus. Come to Jesus, come to the Father – rejoice! Reject Jesus, reject the God who sent him – bad choice.

Advent reminds us just who comes to us, and to whom we come, when we meet Jesus. And we meet Jesus every time we open the Scriptures (5:39). Greet and welcome him with rejoicing today!

Jesus came to give his life (6:32–40, 53–58; 10:10–18). The bread of life, the good shepherd: John's famous images for Jesus both have Advent tones. The bread of life *comes down* from heaven (like the manna did for Israel in the wilderness), and the good shepherd *comes* to provide abundant life for his sheep.

But Jesus transforms both images to speak of his own life *given up in death* so that we might have eternal life. Manna kept people alive – for a while. The broken bread of Jesus' crucified body and his shed blood are 'real food', giving resurrection life to everyone who eats in faith (6:51). Many a lamb lays down its life for food or sacrifice, but only the good shepherd lays down *his* life for his sheep (10:17–18). Advent points us not only to Bethlehem, but also to Calvary. Advent is God coming to be born among us *and* to die for us. And in that too we rejoice.

Jesus came as the model of servant-mission (13:3; 17:13–18; 20:21). 'I don't know whether I'm coming or going', is a cry of confusion or stress or both. Jesus was stressed (Gethsemane), but certainly not confused. And he knew exactly where he had come from and where he was going to (13:3). And it was *because of that* (not in spite of it) that he was secure enough to do the bucket, water and towel thing – a slave's job.

The Lord and Master showed the extent of his love by serving his disciples in the humblest possible posture, down at their feet. Did he kiss them as he dried them, as a woman once showed the extent of her love by doing for him?

A reflection

Advent reaches into the heart of the mission of the Trinity (Father, Son and Holy Spirit). The Father sent the Son, and he came. The Son and the Father sent the Spirit, and he came. And Jesus then extends the divine mission to us: 'As the Father has sent me, so I am sending you,' he said.

What will it mean for you today to live every part of your daily life as someone sent by Christ into the world, as he was?

5

God comes sending us to the nations (act 5)

Bible readings: Luke 24:36–53; Acts 1:1–11

What John Stott taught me in that sermon in [a dark, dilapidated courtyard in] Madras was what his life has taught me ... God so loved the world that the gift of God's Son reorders and enlarges our hearts and our lives.
(Mark Labberton, JS: APBHF, pp. 187, 191)

The whole interim period between Pentecost and the second coming is to be filled with the worldwide mission of the church in the power of the Spirit. Christ's followers were both to announce what he had achieved at his first coming and to summon people to repent and believe in preparation for his second coming. They were to be his witnesses 'to the ends of the earth' (Acts 1:8) and 'to the very end of the age' (Matt. 28:20) ... We have no liberty to stop until both ends have been reached.
(John Stott, BST, *Acts*, p. 45)

*

'Why do all the great missionary texts come at the end of the Gospels?' I used to wonder as a child. My parents were missionaries in Brazil before I was born, and during my childhood my father, as director of his mission agency in Ireland, would speak at missionary meetings where the walls were festooned with banners proclaiming the so-called 'Great Commission' – at the end of Matthew's Gospel.

The other favourite missionary texts came from Mark 16, Luke 24 and John 20. All at the end. Like an afterthought when the main story is finished. It seems like Jesus suddenly wondered what his disciples should do for the rest of their lives, now that he was on his way back to heaven, job done. Why not go and be missionaries? Great idea! Mission seemed like an add-on, to be carried out by special people, missionaries like my dad.

But that is emphatically not the way it is. The mission mandate comes at the end of the Gospels because it is the *climax* of act 4 of the biblical drama, and also the *bridge* that takes us across into act 5. Luke makes these connections between acts 3, 4 and 5 brilliantly in chapter 24.

Do you remember how Jesus spent most of the very first day of his resurrection life? He taught the Old Testament! Twice. First, all afternoon on the road to Emmaus, and then all evening in Jerusalem. Now, I've been a teacher of the Old Testament most of my adult life, and how I wish somebody had recorded those lectures!

'This is what is written,' Jesus said (verse 46). He does not quote an individual text in what follows, but rather sums up the whole of act 3 – 'the Law of Moses, the Prophets and the Psalms' (that's how Jews of Jesus' day referred to what we now call the Old Testament). 'This is what the Scriptures are all about. This is where the whole story so far leads,' he means.

It leads first to the *Messiah*, culminating in his death and resurrection (verse 46) – the whole story of act 4. We rejoice, along with Mary, Zechariah, the angels, the shepherds, Simeon and Anna, in all of God's promises fulfilled . . . the great gospel story is complete! Except that Jesus didn't stop there.

The Old Testament Scriptures of act 3 point *beyond* the resurrection of the Messiah of Israel to the *mission* of Messiah's witnesses. Their task now is to take the good news of repentance and forgiveness to *all* nations (can you hear that echo of Abraham again?). Jesus is telling his disciples (and us) how to read and understand what we now call the Old Testament (verse 45) – with both a messianic *and* a missional meaning. Act 3 points to act 4 (the Messiah), and then act 4 thrusts us forward into act 5 (mission). The story goes on. At one level, for sure, 'it is finished'. On the cross, Christ accomplished God's great plan of redemption. But in another sense, it has only just begun (Acts 1:1).

But what has all this got to do with Advent? Well, Luke actually mentions *two* significant 'comings' in the overlapping final chapter of his Gospel and the first chapter of Acts. These are the two comings that between them embrace the whole of act 5 of the drama. Jesus promises *the coming of the Holy Spirit* (Luke 24:49; Acts 1:8), and angels promise that *Jesus himself will come back* (Acts 1:11). The first promise was fulfilled on the day of Pentecost in Acts 2. We are still waiting for the fulfilment of the second. Act 5 is everything in between. So that is where we are now, living somewhere between Jesus' ascension and his return, somewhere between Pentecost and the second coming.

Now here's the thing: that means *we are in the Bible story!* Did you ever realize that? Well, you are! We are participating in act 5 of the great drama of Scripture, playing our part in the mission of God until Christ returns to inaugurate acts 6 and 7.

This turns inside out the way we usually think about the Bible in relation to our own lives. We talk about 'applying the Bible to my life', as if 'my life' were the key story and the Bible somehow has to fit into it. But it's the other way round. We should ask, 'How does my life fit into the great story of the Bible? How do I play my part in the purpose and plan of God, "in the meantime" between the first and second comings of Jesus Christ?'

That's Advent thinking, and I reckon you'll find it's thoroughly missional and practical.

It's missional because the coming of the Holy Spirit at Pentecost was explicitly to empower Christ's followers to bear witness to him. Now, of course, the Spirit of God has been active in many ways through the Old Testament since Genesis 1:2. But at Pentecost there was a unique outpouring of the Spirit on *all* believers. The church in mission needs the power and direction and gifts and fruit of the Spirit of the risen Christ – as Luke will show repeatedly in the rest of the book of Acts. So think about Advent as a summons to mission – for all of us.

And it's practical because we are called to shape our lives ethically in the light of Christ's past and future advents, or, as Paul puts it in his letter to Titus, between his two 'appearings' – past and future (Titus 2:11–14). So think about Advent as a summons to live in hope and in holiness until Christ returns.

A prayer

Fill me this day with your Holy Spirit, Lord Jesus Christ, so that I may have power to bear witness to you, patience in waiting for your return, and perseverance in the good works which you prepared for me to walk in.

6

God comes to put things right (act 6)

Bible readings: Matthew 25:31–46; John 5:24–29

From John Stott:

> I am not naturally a weepy person, and am generally regarded as strong . . . But [when] I read the Gospels, I discovered that Jesus our Lord is recorded as having wept in public twice . . . So, if Jesus wept, his disciples may presumably do so also.
> (TRD, p. 105)

> We see the malice, cruelty, power and arrogance of the evil men who persecute. We see also the sufferings of the people of God, who are opposed, ridiculed, boycotted, harassed, imprisoned, tortured and killed – the wicked flourishing and the righteous suffering . . .
> 'Why doesn't God do something?' we complain indignantly. And the answer is that he is doing something and will go on doing it. He is allowing his people to suffer, in order to qualify them for his heavenly kingdom. He is allowing the wicked to triumph temporarily, but his just judgment will fall upon them in the end. Thus Paul sees evidence that God's judgment is right in the very situation in which we might see nothing but injustice.
> (BST, *Thessalonians*, p. 147)

*

'Justice has been done at last. Now we can sleep again.' Heart-breaking words from a news bulletin, as bereaved relatives stand outside a court where the convicted murderer has been found guilty and received a maximum sentence. 'Of course,' they may add, 'nothing can bring our daughter back. But at least he will pay for his crime and the suffering it has caused us.' And that offers some small measure of peace to their grieving hearts.

So hard to hear, and yet it resonates with a conviction deeply rooted in our personal and social conscience, that deliberately evil acts demand some appropriate measure of punishment. Some-how, somewhere, we feel, intentional wrongdoing should be paid for.

This is not merely a malicious lust for vengeance (though it so easily slides down into that vortex of violence). It is, rather, the longing to see justice done. Sin and wrongdoing have consequences – must have, or God's a liar, the Bible's a fiction and the universe is a moral chaos. Things must be put right – even though we know, like the bereaved parents, that some things can never be put right in this life, even by the strictest exercise of our limited human justice systems.

Not in this life, perhaps, but does that mean for ever not? That possibility frustrates and angers those who don't believe in any-thing beyond 'this life'. 'He cheated justice,' we hear, when some perpetrator of terrible evils dies without ever being caught and made to pay. It's just *not fair* that they 'got away with it'. That kind of impunity – never being called to account for the consequences of one's wrongdoing – is a terrible evil in itself, and seems to release the worst horrors that our fallen human nature is capable of. Where there is no likelihood of punishment for wrong, there are no limits to our potential for evil.

But the question returns: will evildoers 'get away with it' for ever? The Bible cries out from God's throne, 'No!' There will be no eternal impunity. Evil will not have the last word. Act 6 of the biblical drama lies ahead: the day of judgment, the day of final reckoning and total rectification. It is an essential and integral part of the whole Bible story. And it is good that it is.

The Old Testament prophets called it the Day of the Lord, when God will deal with his enemies (though, painfully, they recognized that Israel itself had fallen into that category and faced God's judgment). Jesus spoke of 'that day' (Matthew 7:22), and his parables portray the stark division it will expose among people and the stark contrast in their destinies – raised into eternal life, or condemnation (John 5:29). Paul likewise anticipates 'the day when God judges people's secrets through Jesus Christ, as my gospel declares' (Romans 2:16).

'Go to the naughty step!' Our four-year-old grandson is exiled from our company by his parents, and the door shut. After three minutes are up, the door opens and the crestfallen wee lad returns to a familiar ritual. 'What did you do?'

'I hit my brother.'

'And what do you say?'

'Sorry, Joseph.'

'And what do you say, Joseph?'

'That's OK.' Hugs and tears (sometimes).

Wrongdoing, punishment, repentance, forgiveness. A minuscule enactment of the gospel – but with one massive difference. The cost of our sin was carried by God himself in the person of his sinless Son, made sin for us on the cross. And so the day of judgment holds no terrors, even for the wickedest perpetrator of wrong *who repents and turns back to God in faith and obedience*. For, as Ezekiel affirmed about somebody he portrays as an idolater, adulterer, robber, oppressor and exploiter (in breathtaking words):

> If someone who is wicked repents, that person's former wickedness will not bring condemnation . . . None of the sins that person has committed will be remembered against them . . . 'As surely as I live, declares the Sovereign LORD, I take no pleasure in the death of the wicked, but rather that they turn from their ways and live.' . . . Repent and live!
> (Ezekiel 33:12, 16, 11; 18:32)

But what if there is no repentance? With tragic realism, the Bible anticipates that some will never repent, indeed will refuse to repent (Revelation 9:20–21). What then for those who refuse to obey the gospel? Paul tells us (in 2 Thessalonians 1:8–10). The door to God's presence and glory, for ever shut. Grim indeed.

And yet Paul refers to 'that day' as *part of the gospel* (Romans 2:16). Why? Because it is indeed good news that God will not allow evil to have the last word in God's universe. Unrepentant evildoers will not 'get away with it' for ever. When the accumulated arrogance, corruption and violence of humanity – all that is represented by 'Babylon' – is finally brought low and destroyed, all of creation will explode with praise and joy and reverberating 'Hallelujahs' (Revelation 18 – 19). The ultimate overthrow of evil has to be good news!

The Judge of all the earth will do what is right (Genesis 18:25). And he is the God of infinite justice and infinite mercy. One day all wrongs will be put right – including those that could never be put right in any meaningful way in this life. That is the promise, the miracle and the anticipated joy of God's advent in act 6. God comes to judge the earth, and all creation will rejoice (Psalm 96:10–13).

God will put all things right. And then he will make all things new.

A prayer
Almighty God, like you, I take no pleasure in the judgment of the wicked. Yet I rejoice to know that you are the utterly just Judge of all the earth, and you will put all things right in your creation. Please let my life and my words bear witness to your saving love in Christ, so that others may come to repentance and salvation before that day, for Jesus Christ's sake. Amen.

7

God comes creating a whole new world (act 7)

Bible reading: Isaiah 60

John Stott believed that there will be a new creation in which
we may all share through repentance and faith in Jesus.
(Frances Whitehead, John Stott's secretary for fifty-five years,
Thanksgiving tribute)

The promise of a new heaven and a new earth was first made
by God to Isaiah (65:17–25; 66:22). Jesus himself spoke of it as
'the renewal of all things' (Matt. 19:28), and Paul wrote of it
as creation's liberation from its bondage to decay (Rom. 8:21).

It is important therefore to affirm that our Christian hope
looks forward not to an ethereal heaven, but a renewed
universe, related to the present world by both continuity and
discontinuity . . . the new heaven and the new earth will not
be a replacement universe (as if created *de novo*), but a
regenerated universe, purged of all present imperfections,
with no more pain, sin or death.
(John Stott, TIC, p. 224)

*

When at last we reach that final episode of our television drama, we
often find that there were hints and clues to the final denouement
all along, with visual flashbacks to help us see the connections.

And so it is when we reach the last act of the great biblical drama:
act 7 and the new creation. The closing chapters of the Bible, Revelation 21 – 22, are saturated in imagery that we have seen many times

before – that is, if we were watching carefully through the earlier acts. So today, let's savour Isaiah's kaleidoscope of images of God's future.

Can you see the three great 'comings' in chapter 60?

First, the light of God is coming to his people (verses 1–2). Even after the return from exile, the people of Israel were sinful and disobedient. Isaiah 59 portrays this as disabling and depressing darkness – a painful picture of social evil (59:8–15). But God is on his way! Israel's Redeemer is coming for the repentant (59:17, 20).

So, in chapter 60, verses 1–2 prophetically describe God's arrival as if it had already happened – the light of God's glory dawns over God's people. Maybe you're more familiar with Isaiah 9:2. I'm sure you'll soon hear this text being read in a carol service:

The people walking in darkness
   have seen a great light;
on those living in the land of deep darkness
   a light has dawned.

Those words lead us straight to Christmas and the birth of a Child, the Son, on that night when the light of glory shone briefly in Bethlehem's fields. But by the end of our chapter, Isaiah foresees the *everlasting* light of God's presence, outshining the sun in God's new creation (verses 19–20; Revelation 21:23; 22:5). Christ's first advent would bring God's light into the *world's* darkness (not just Israel's). For the Messiah of Israel is for the nations of the whole world – 'the earth' and 'the peoples', 'nations' and 'kings' (verses 2–3). And that's where we go next.

Second, peoples of the world are coming to God (verses 3–16). Light is attractive – ask any moth. For years I lived in a house surrounded by woodland. As I drove home at night, I loved the moment when I could see the lights of my home twinkling through the dark trees, drawing me in by their welcome. So, if the light is shining in and through God's people, Isaiah sees the nations being drawn towards that light, coming out of their alienation and darkness to worship the living God (just like Isaiah 2:1–5).

What will that look like? Only poetic imagination can express something beyond easy description. The prophet's words were intended first of all to encourage the exiles of Judah returning to their land, but his poetry soars to heights that far outstrip that historical reality alone. Remember, these verses (3–16) are highly pictorial, not literalistic. We need to feel their emotional impact as a vision of the future, not analyse every image and look for literal 'fulfilment'.

The nations will come bringing Israel's *sons and daughters* (verses 4, 9). But who are they going to be? Psalm 87 tells us that people of many nations will be counted as native-born citizens of Zion. And as the gospel went out to the Gentile nations in the New Testament, Paul told the Galatian believers that, through faith in Christ, they too, along with believing Jews, were sons of Abraham (Galatians 3:7–9, 26–29).

The nations will come bringing their *gifts* (verses 5–7, 11). The prophet sees gifts from the West (the seas) and from the East (Midian and Sheba) – just as the Magi (or wise men) brought their gifts to Jesus, and Paul brought the offering of the Gentiles to Jerusalem as a symbolic fulfilment. Kedar and Nebaioth were sons of Ishmael (verse 7; Genesis 25:13). Even the Arab tribes will join in the worship of the living God. For that is ultimately what the nations are coming to do.

The nations will come bringing their *worship*, praising God and adorning his temple (verses 6, 7b, 9b, 13). The new creation needs its population: a multitude from every tribe and nation united in the worship of the Lord, the Saviour, the Redeemer, the Mighty One of Jacob (verse 16), and walking in his light.

Third, peace and justice are coming to the world (verses 17–22). The prophet has portrayed, first, something which we know has already happened (verses 1–2): the light of God's salvation which arrived with Jesus Christ (act 4). And then, he has pictured something that is even now ongoing (verses 3–16): people from many nations coming to know and worship the living God of Israel, through the mission of the church (act 5). So now, at last, he pictures something yet to come, when the world itself will be transformed.

There's a whole new world coming! And we have to use our imaginations (like 65:17–25). It will be a world

- of perfect peace and justice;
- without violence or destruction;
- filled with the light of God's own presence;
- where people live in perfect righteousness and everlasting security;
- filled to overflowing with God's own beauty and splendour.

Rejoice? How could we do otherwise!

I am the LORD;
  in its time I will do this swiftly.
(verse 22)

Amen. Come, Lord Jesus!

A reflection

'Arise, shine, for your light has come' (Isaiah 60:1). The opening verse is a summons, a command.

What does it mean to shine with the light of God? Isaiah has already explained: by living in a way that reflects the justice and compassion of God himself (Isaiah 58:6–10). Was Jesus thinking of those verses when he said to his disciples, 'You are the light of the world' (Matthew 5:14), and told them to let their light shine by *doing good*?

Whenever we sing, 'Shine, Jesus, shine', I seem to hear a voice from heaven urging, 'Shine yourselves, why don't you?'

Week 2

THE GOD WHO CAME IN PERSON

Advent reminds us of the God who has come, comes, and will come again.

In the Bible, the outstandingly dominant note is that God comes to save. Of course, God's salvation will involve judgment, as we have seen. God must deal with evil for salvation to have any meaning or permanence. But salvation is what God most often comes to accomplish. After all, that's why they called his name Jesus: Ye[ho]shua, 'The Lord is salvation'.

So, after an opening psalm that celebrates our saving God, we will spend the rest of this week in a single biblical book, one that describes God's greatest act of salvation, second only to the cross of Christ: the book of Exodus.

Exodus tells a gripping story. It begins with a situation that resonates with some of the horrors of our world today. We see an ethnic immigrant minority people being cynically scapegoated as objects of political fear and hatred, and then ruthlessly exploited economically and subjected to state-sponsored genocide. God hears their cry and resolves to act on their behalf. From then on, God comes repeatedly as the real central hero of the story – saving, speaking, covenanting, instructing, camping, forgiving and leading his people.

And through all these close encounters, God reveals himself – his power, his justice, his compassion, his holiness and, above all, his name, Yahweh, the LORD God. This is God in person, not just a 'force'. This is God on earth, not just 'up in heaven'. This is God up close, not far off – though, paradoxically, people who draw near to him need to keep a respectful distance.

But we begin with a psalmist who needed to apply the great saving truths of the exodus story to the stresses of his own life. Perhaps you need to do the same today and this week. I invite you, or rather the Bible itself invites you, to make the words of trust and confidence of Psalm 62 your own. For the God of David is our God still.

A prayer for week 2 of Advent

Blessed Lord, you caused all holy Scriptures to be written for our learning. Help us so to hear them, to read, mark, learn and inwardly digest them, so that, through patience, and the comfort of your holy word, we may embrace and for ever hold fast the hope of everlasting life, which you have given us in our Saviour Jesus Christ. Amen.

8

My Rock and my salvation

Bible reading: Psalm 62

From John Stott:

> The believer's faith is grounded upon who God is . . . He is the
> believer's refuge and fortress.
> (FP, p. 81)

> Nothing seems stable in our world any longer. Insecurity is
> written across all human experience. Christians are not guar-
> anteed immunity to temptation, tribulation or tragedy, but
> we are promised victory over them. God's pledge is not that
> suffering will never afflict us, but that it will never separate
> us from his love . . . Our confidence is not in our love for him,
> which is frail, fickle and faltering, but in his love for us, which
> is steadfast, faithful and persevering.
> (BST, *Romans*, p. 259)

*

> Hear what comfortable words our Saviour Christ saith unto
> all who truly turn to him: 'Come unto me, all ye that labour
> and are heavy-laden, and *I will refresh you.*'
> (Book of Common Prayer, emphasis added)

When I was a curate in Tonbridge Parish Church in the late 1970s,
I loved speaking those beautiful words from the Anglican service
of Holy Communion according to the Book of Common Prayer. I
would put special slow emphasis on those concluding words. They
carry such a depth of promise. Like a glass of cold water for the dry,

weary and thirsty soul – *'I will refresh you!'* They are indeed 'comfortable' or strengthening words.

David starts in that tone of voice:

> Truly, my soul finds rest in God;
>   my salvation comes from him.

Finding rest in God. Maybe you can identify with the pressure and stress David feels. There is the external stress of mockery and hostility (verses 3–4), and the internal stress of the imbalance and injustice he sees in society around him (verses 9–10). Isn't that what many of us face in our contemporary culture and workplaces? So he speaks to his own soul – taking himself in hand, as it were (as in Psalms 42 – 43) – and challenges himself to find his stress-busting rest in God. He begins with a small but emphatic word of exclamation – which could mean *'only* in God' or *'truly* in God'. The cunning translators of the old KJV manage to get both senses across: *'Truly* my soul waiteth upon God . . . He *only* is my rock and my salvation.'

This is strongly relational language. Note the repeated 'my' (verses 6–7): *my* salvation, *my* rock, *my* fortress, *my* hope, *my* honour. But it is also community language, for these words are filled with Israel's story. 'Salvation' speaks of the exodus. 'Rest' speaks of the gift of the Promised Land. David is making the story of his own people the confession of his own soul. If God can do that for *Israel*, he can do that for *me* too. And then in verse 8, David turns it all back to the people again. What God has done for *me* ('my soul'), he can do for *you* ('you people'). Whether me or you, the message is the same: 'Trust in him at all times . . . for God is *our* refuge.' Rest and rejoice in that today.

Finding rest in the midst of conflict. David voices the relational stress of leadership. Even as anointed king, he is surrounded by conspiracies, lies, threats – actual or suspected. He feels like a tottering wall (verses 3–4). One more push and . . .

Maybe you too know something of that, in your place of work, even in your church, or in the vulnerability of Christian leadership.

Being constantly 'got at', being the victim, or painted as the villain in some conflict, can be dreadfully draining, emotionally and spiritually. What do we do with it? There is a proper place, of course, for competent pastoral care and accountability. But in the last extremity there is only one place to go for 'rest' – 'in God alone'. Why?

'My salvation and *my honour* depend on God.' Verse 7 helps, I think. Whatever my reputation may suffer, God knows the truth. He will vindicate me – if that is needed. Or he will correct me – if that is needed. But I can rest, refresh and strengthen myself in the security of the God who looks on the heart.

That's how Jesus reacted. 'When they hurled their insults at him, he did not retaliate; when he suffered, he made no threats. Instead, he entrusted himself to him who judges justly' (1 Peter 2:23). Peter means that we should do the same.

Finding rest in the midst of corruption (verses 9–10). David looks out and sees the same broken realities that we know very well in our own land. There is social stratification (verse 9) – the 'elite' and the 'forgotten'. There is extortion and theft (verse 10a) – now on a global scale. And there is the tendency and temptation of riches increasing (verse 10b): while the poor stay poor, the rich get richer.

Do these social evils make you upset, envious, angry? What do you do when such emotions surge up inside? David responds by 'resting' in two deep truths about God (verses 11–12).

First, both power *and* unfailing love belong to God. He is characterized by both – not just one or the other. If God were all power but no love, that would be utterly scary. But if God were all loving and had no power, that would be pathetic. No, David affirms the God of the exodus, who demonstrated the *power* of his *love*. The cross of Christ demonstrates the same truth to its infinite degree.

Second, that God will indeed put all things right with perfect justice (verse 12b). He will deal with and rectify the injustices that make him, and us, so angry. And that, as we saw last week, is part of the good news of the gospel. The evildoers who afflicted David will not 'get away with it' for ever.

The gracious balance of Scripture

That very last line of the psalm, however, is only partly true. For David was aware that, in the case of those who repent of their evil doings (as he did) and trust in God's forgiveness (as he did), God does *not* 'reward everyone according to what they have done'. On the contrary, in his mercy and grace, '[God] does *not* treat us as our sins deserve or repay us according to our iniquities' (Psalm 103:10). This is just as well, for otherwise,

If you, LORD, kept a record of sins,
    LORD, who could stand?
But with you there is forgiveness.
(Psalm 130:3–4)

'Comfortable words' indeed, spoken to us not just by David, but by the invitation of none other than the crucified Christ himself.

9

God comes to the rescue

Bible reading: Exodus 2:23 – 3:10

John Stott was powerfully persuaded by the capacity of Christians to change society.
(David Turner, JS: APBHF, p. 85)

The law and the prophets, Jesus and his apostles, all lay on us a particular duty to serve the poor and defend the powerless. We cannot escape this by saying they are not our responsibility. We need, then, to feel the pain of those who suffer oppression. 'Remember those in prison as if you were their fellow-prisoners, and those who are mistreated as if you yourselves were suffering' (Hebrews 13.3).
(John Stott, IFCT, p. 206)

*

I must have been yelling pretty loudly. I had been let out to play in a farmyard in Northern Ireland. I decided to scramble up a monster pile of pig manure, which must have seemed like a mini-Everest to my three-year-old curiosity. The crust at the top gave way, however, and I began to sink – and stink – until the slurry was swallowing my shiny new red wellies and threatening to swallow me with them. Perhaps not quite life threatening, but very stuck I was and very scared. My dad came running out to rescue me, with a mighty hand and an outstretched arm, and at no little cost to his own clothing, dignity and aroma!

Israel's cries went up (2:23) and Israel's God came down (3:8). That, in a nutshell, is the advent event that launches the epic narrative of Exodus.

Like me, as a child, you probably learned the stories of Pharaoh and the Hebrew slaves, bricks without straw, Moses in the bulrushes and all that. The trouble is, those stories can stay in that childhood memory, Bible storybook form, long into adulthood. We now need to read Exodus 1 with adult eyes that have watched real-life suffering in the news bulletins of our cruel world. For then we will recognize only too painfully the acute agony and bondage of the Hebrews, with all its jagged dimensions still crushing millions today.

Politically, the Hebrews were an immigrant ethnic minority who had come originally as famine refugees, welcomed by a previous government, but were now being stigmatized as a threat. *Economically*, they were subjected to the ruthless exploitation of their labour, all for the benefit of the construction needs of the host nation – in back-breaking brick kilns, where, incidentally, thousands of slaves still sweat even today. *Socially*, they became victims of a state-sponsored campaign of genocide. And *spiritually*, their servitude to the usurped deity, Pharaoh, has all but obliterated (and certainly severely hindered) their worship of the One who had been their true God ('serve' and 'worship' are the same word in Hebrew). No wonder they groaned, sighed and cried out under their unbearable suffering (verse 23).

But enter God.

God bursts into the text with an emphatic response that takes four verbs to express: '*God* heard . . . *God* remembered . . . *God* saw . . . and *God* knew' (2:24, ESV). Human realities are turned upside down. *The Israelites* may think their suffering is invisible in heaven. *The Egyptians* may think their injustice is beyond retribution. *Moses* may think his exiled status rules him out of the game altogether. But God is on the case; God is on his way. God comes to the rescue. Advent hope blooms.

God knows how to get attention – even the attention of an octogenarian whose eyes had only been watching sheep for forty years. A bush on fire but not consumed, and a human-like figure wrapped in flames speaking from inside it. That'd do it. God identifies himself as the God of Abraham (3:6; remember that promise last week?), and then we get another four rapid-fire verbs all with God speaking for himself: 'I have seen . . . I have heard . . . I know . . . I have come down to rescue . . .' (3:7–9).

So God steps in to accomplish the first act of *redemption* in the Bible (and the greatest until the cross). The exodus is explicitly described as God 'redeeming' (6:6; 15:13), and the name of Yahweh as 'Redeemer' will for ever be linked with this great historical act.

How big is your idea of 'redemption'? Well, here is redemption on God's terms. Can you see how God addresses all four of those dimensions of Israel's bondage? *Politically*, God liberates them from the realm and power of Pharaoh's empire. *Economically*, God frees them from exploitation and slavery to give them a land of their own to work and share in its bounty. *Socially*, God frees them from genocide and gives them a constitution with a whole range of rights and responsibilities for a healthy society. And *spiritually*, God brings them into covenant relationship with himself, in which they *know* who the living God, *their* God, truly is (6:7).

This is God's idea of redemption on a comprehensive scale. It includes justice, compassion, promise keeping, salvation, deep personal relationship and God's determination to be *known* as God of all the earth (9:13–16).

Now we don't go out into the world to engineer exoduses. Our mission is not to play at being God. But the exodus constantly inspired and mandated Old Testament Israel (through the law and prophets) to exercise justice for the oppressed and compassion for the poor, as part of 'knowing God' in acceptable worship. Our mission also must surely have some exodus-shaped dimensions that reflect the heart of God as revealed in this narrative. The God of Moses is the God and Father of our Lord Jesus Christ. And he is still the God who hears and sees and knows . . . *and sends*.

Don't you think Moses' heart was filling with joy as he listened to God? God *has* seen it all! He is coming to the rescue! Good for God! Until verse 10. 'So now, go. *I am sending you . . . !*' The shock reverberates through the disbelief and desperation of five objections before it sinks in. God will not accomplish his mission alone. But then, neither will Moses. *'I will be with you'* (verse 12). They are in this together, just as whatever mission God calls us into flows

43

from the mission of God himself. Truly, 'we go not forth alone against the foe'.

A prayer

'Let my heart be broken by the things that break the heart of God' was the prayer of Bob Pierce, founder of World Vision, after witnessing first-hand the suffering and poverty of children. His prayer assumes that God *feels* the pain of human suffering in his own inner being – his 'heart'. As Isaiah says about God's response to the Israelites in Egypt,

> *In all their affliction he was afflicted,*
>   and the angel of his presence saved them;
> in his love and in his pity he redeemed them.
> (Isaiah 63:9, ESV)

10

God comes to speak

Bible readings: Exodus 19:1–9, 16–19; 20:18–21

From John Stott:

> 'Please Lord, I want to see some "wonderful things" in your
> word.'
> But God may reply, 'What makes you think I have only
> "wonderful things" to show you? As a matter of fact, I have
> some rather "disturbing things" to show you today. Are you
> prepared to receive them?'
> (TB, TCC series, p. 41)

> It is not enough to *possess* a Bible . . . to *read* the Bible . . . to
> *study* the Bible. Some Christians . . . have read it many times
> from cover to cover and committed large sections to memory.
> No. What is required is that we *obey* the Bible. The best way to
> honour this book as God's book is to do what it says. And if we
> do [this], we shall keep coming to Christ for the supply of all
> our needs.
> (BISTY, pp. 103–104)

*

What's the most spectacularly awesome sight you have ever wit-
nessed? A New Year's Eve fireworks display? The Northern Lights?
A ferocious tropical thunderstorm? Sunrise or sunset among
snow-capped mountain peaks? The launch of a space rocket?

But such phenomena feel like a whisper beside what happened at Mount Sinai.

Imagine yourself there. Your eyes, when not blinded by streaks of lightning, are scanning a dense cloud, but cannot penetrate the thick darkness within it; your ears are bursting with thunderclaps and the crescendo of a descending trumpet blast; your feet can feel the mountain itself quaking beneath you; your nose and mouth are assaulted with fire and smoke. No wonder 'everyone in the camp trembled' (19:16). Wouldn't you?

The technical word for such an event is a 'theophany' – an 'appearance of God'. But 'advent' would be a better term, since God did not just 'appear' – God *came* (19:9; 20:20), or he *came down* (19:11, 18, 20). And when God comes, stuff happens – though not always stuff on this scale (thankfully!). And what happened had an impact not only on creation for a short time, but also on Israel's memory and worship for ever. As always, however, God's coming is for a purpose – or in this case, for two purposes. God gives us one (19:9) and Moses gives us the other (20:20).

God comes in order to be heard (19:9). God tells Moses that he is coming not just to be seen, but to be heard. The people are amazed to witness God in conversation with Moses: 'Moses was speaking and God was answering him with a voice' (verse 11, my translation). At that moment the content of God's direct speech consists of the Ten Commandments (20:1–17). Yahweh is *the God who speaks*, to reveal his person, his plans, his ways and his guidance. Where does God speak today? Through his word in Scripture and his living Word in Christ. Advent reminds us that *God comes to communicate*. We should not need phenomena like Mount Sinai to be ready to listen.

God comes in order to be feared (20:20). Well, after what we read in chapter 19, the people's reaction was hardly surprising (20:18–19). But Moses' reply is surprising. He tells them *not* to fear because God wanted them to fear! What he meant was: they need not fear the fiery *mountain*; they need to fear the living *God*. But that is only so that they might be kept from sinning, and so live and prosper.

Fear him, ye saints, and you will then
Have nothing else to fear.[1]

Moses later recalls that this was the longing in God's own heart at
this moment. 'Oh, that their hearts would be inclined to fear me
and keep all my commands always, *so that it might go well with them
and their children for ever!*' (Deuteronomy 5:29; see also Deuteronomy 5:22–33 for Moses' own memory of this scene).

'Do you *hear* me, Christopher?' my mother would say sternly.
'Yes, Mum,' I'd mumble. 'Then *heed* me!' she would warn, with
emphatic articulation – for my own good, of course. 'Hear and
heed' – very closely connected, as in our passage. Israel should *hear
God and fear God*, by trusting his word and obeying his voice, for
their own good. Reflect for a moment. What word is God speaking
into your life this Advent? Are you hearing and heeding him?

As soon as Israel reached Mount Sinai, God told Moses what to
say to the Israelites (19:1–6). And this speech comes *before* God
gives the Ten Commandments and the rest of his laws for Israel.
And that timing is vital.

First of all, God points back to the *past*, the great saving act of
God which they had just lived through. 'You have seen what I have
done . . .' Indeed they had. Three months ago, suffering slaves;
today, a freed people. God took the initiative in his love and grace.
He acted first, and only then called on the people to obey his law in
response. God saved them first, and then called on them to respond
in obedience. And that's how it is for us too. Grace first – then, now
and always. Obedience as grateful response. 'We love, because God
first loved us' (1 John 4:19), 'forgiving each other, just as in Christ
God forgave you' (Ephesians 4:32).

God looks to the *future* too. Can you hear those echoes of
Abraham again, when God speaks of 'the whole earth' and 'all
nations'? After all, here was the very spot where God had identified
himself to Moses as the God of Abraham. God had a unique role
for Israel in his plan for the blessing of *all* nations on earth. It's as if

---

1 Nicholas Brady and Nahum Tate, 'Through All the Changing Scenes of Life', 1696.

God can see them all from the top of Mount Sinai. He knows where this story began (with his promise to Abraham), and where it is going (to the ends of the earth).

So what about the *present*, then? How must Israel live now, if God wants them to be his priestly and holy people in the midst of the nations? They will need to live in grateful obedience to the pattern of life that God is about to give them in his covenant law (19:5–6). God comes to give his laws to people with a past (redeemed by God's grace) and a future (for God's mission to all nations).

An exercise

Turn to 1 Peter 2:9–12. How much of it is directly connected to Exodus 19:3–6? How does Peter apply to us as Christian believers the identity, the experience and the responsibilities that God gave to Old Testament Israel? How is God's past grace in your life affecting how you now live, and what you're living for?

11

God comes for a meal

Bible reading: Exodus 24:1–11

From John Stott:

> It is our common participation in God (Father, Son and Spirit) which unites us. And this is most vividly expressed in the Lord's Supper.
> (TLC, p. 97)

> One evening in an upper room in Jerusalem a Galilean peasant, carpenter by trade and preacher by vocation, dared to say in effect: 'this new covenant, prophesied by Jeremiah (Jer. 31:31–34), is about to be established; the forgiveness of sins promised as one of its distinctive blessings is about to become available; and the sacrifice to seal this covenant and procure this forgiveness will be the shedding of my blood in death.'
> Is it possible to exaggerate the staggering nature of this claim?
> (TCOC, pp. 69–70)

*

Few things are more enjoyable than a good meal in cheerful company with friends and family. At least I think so, and hope you agree! God certainly does.

God loves meals with people. Jesus spent so much of his precious time eating and drinking with people that he got a reputation for it. In fact, food in all its infinite variety is part of God's joyful gift in creation. 'At the beginning of the Bible story, the first thing God does for humanity is present us with a menu . . . (Genesis 2:8–9) . . . God thinks food is a good thing.'[1]

Remember how God renewed his promise to Abraham and Sarah over a leisurely afternoon lunch? Then the exodus was marked by a hasty night-time family meal, the Passover – and has been celebrated that way by Jews ever since. Today we see how God sealed his covenant with his people by having their representatives enjoy a meal in his gracious presence on a mountainside where heaven and earth briefly met (verse 10).

But before the meal, the ceremony. God has come down to Sinai, and Moses has received the first instalment of God's instructions for his redeemed people (chapters 19 – 23). The covenant relationship must now be ratified.

Let's just pick out two important moments in the story.

Sacrifice and sprinkling (verses 4–8). The action with the sacrificial blood – sprinkling half on the altar and half on the people – is unusual. The only other time it happens like this is at the ordination of Aaron and his sons as priests (29:19–21). Which suggests that here in chapter 24 we have the consecration of Israel as a whole to be God's priestly people in the midst of the nations (19:5–6).

Moses sprinkles half the blood on the people, however, only *after* three things have happened:

1 Burnt offerings and fellowship offerings have been sacrificed, and half the blood splashed on the altar, representing God. This speaks of the atoning grace of God accepting the people into covenant fellowship with himself and one another.
2 The words of God, recorded on the scroll, have been read out, so that the people know what it will mean to live as the people of this God. They are to worship Yahweh alone, and to imitate the justice and compassion of their Redeemer God in their social life as a nation (chapters 20 – 23).
3 The people have repeated for the third time that they are willing to do all that God required (19:8; 24:3, 7). So they accept the

1 Tim Chester, *A Meal with Jesus* (IVP, 2011), p. 70.

ethical responsibility of being his priestly and holy people. Of course, we know (and God knew) that they would not live up to it, but it is important that they did intentionally make that commitment as their side of the covenant. Even broken commitments will matter.

Being sprinkled with 'the blood of the covenant', then, meant they were a people *accepted by God's grace, acquainted with God's word* and *committed to God's ways.*

What do those three phrases mean in your life? For if we have been redeemed and 'sprinkled' by the blood of our Lord Jesus Christ, then they are true for us too.

'This is my blood of the covenant, which is poured out for many for the forgiveness of sins,' said Jesus, as he ate that last Passover meal with his disciples (Matthew 26:28). His words reflect not only 'the blood of the covenant' in Exodus 24, but also two other prophetic scriptures that interpret his death. The words 'poured out for many' evoke the vicarious suffering and death of the Servant of the Lord (Isaiah 53:11–12). And the words 'for the forgiveness of sins' recall the climax of Jeremiah's vision of the new covenant (Jeremiah 31:34).

The death of Christ has given us believers not only our 'exodus', but also our 'Sinai'. Rejoice today in God's redemption and God's covenant. And check out how Hebrews in the New Testament encourages us with the benefits of Christ's sprinkled blood (Hebrews 9:19–22; 10:22).

Seeing and eating (verses 9–11). 'They saw God, and they ate and drank' (verse 11). Are you as surprised as I was when I first came across that verse? We might have expected that they saw God and were transfixed with joy, or prostrate with fear, or 'lost in wonder, love and praise'. But no, they saw God (!), and got out the picnic baskets (perhaps meat from the fellowship offerings), and 'they ate and drank'. That's all. Beautiful! God loves a good meal among friends.

And what did they see? The writer knows that nobody can literally see God as he truly is. So he hints mysteriously that they saw only 'God's feet' through a translucent sky-blue platform. Heaven comes to earth. Advent in the sky with sapphires. Three disciples saw something of that glory in the dazzling white of the transfiguration of Jesus. Many others 'saw God and ate and drank' in those Gospel meals where Jesus did some of his most God-like work, seeking and saving the lost. Good for them.

But what about us?

Will we ever truly see God and eat and drink in his presence? Well, to some extent, in the Lord's Supper. But Isaiah portrays a much greater mountain-top meal, laid on by God himself, and with a guest list infinitely larger than seventy-four geriatric mountaineers. It will be nothing less than a banquet for all the nations, in which God will personally stoop to wipe the tears from the faces of his guests. Take a look (Isaiah 25:6–8). Could anything be more intimate?

Isn't that a meal to look forward to?

A prayer

I rejoice, Lord, along with all those around the world who have received your invitation to the wedding banquet of the Lamb (Revelation 19:6–9), and I look forward eagerly to that day. Help me today, wherever I may eat and drink, to do so in your presence, invited by the sacrifice and new covenant blood of your Son, our Lord Jesus Christ. Amen.

12

God comes to stay

Bible readings: Exodus 25:1–8; 29:42–46

From John Stott:

> The ideal is beautiful. The church is the chosen and beloved people of God, his own special treasure, the covenant community to whom he has committed himself for ever. It is engaged in continuous worship of God and in compassionate outreach to the world, a haven of love and peace, and a pilgrim people headed for the eternal city.
> (TC, TCC series, p. 9)

> The new temple . . . is neither a material building nor a national shrine, nor has it a localized site. It is a spiritual building (God's household) and an international community (embracing Gentiles as well as Jews), and it has a worldwide spread (wherever God's people are to be found). This is where God dwells. He is not tied to holy buildings, but to holy people, to his own new society. To them he has pledged himself by a solemn covenant. He lives in them, individually and as a community.
> (BST, *Ephesians*, p. 109)

*

'Don't be scared,' our eight-year-old daughter whispered to her brothers on the other side of the partition in our canvas tent on our first night camping out in the forest. 'God can still see us, just as easily here as back home or in church.'

She was right, of course. God rather likes tents. In fact, he reminded David that he (God) had been perfectly happy dwelling in his tent for hundreds of years before David had the idea of building him a house, which God didn't really need anyway (2 Samuel 7:5–7). The story of that tent ('the tabernacle') takes us back to Mount Sinai.

As we saw yesterday, there was a moment at Mount Sinai when heaven and earth met as God 'came down'. The mountain became a kind of vertical temple, bringing God together with his people through their mediator (Moses) and the blood of sacrifice. Holiness and grace combine. The people see the glory of God in cloud and fire from a safe distance; their representatives eat and drink unharmed in his presence; and Moses alone goes into the most holy presence of God at the mountain top.

The thing about mountains, though, is that they don't tend to move much, whereas God's people are very much on the move in this story. So is there any way the mountain-top experience of God's presence can become not just a once-in-a-lifetime experience for the elders to tell the grandchildren about, but an ongoing, permanently available reality for the whole people as they journey on? Yes, says God. And here's how. We come to another of those jaw-dropping surprises.

What would you say the exodus story so far has told us about God? Surely it must be that he is simply awesome (in the proper sense of that much-trivialized word). Think of his victory over the Egyptian empire, his cosmic power over all creation, including the wind and the sea, his earth-shaking, fiery holiness. So, with bated breath, we watch as Moses enters right into that awesome presence (24:18). What will this cosmically fearsome God say or do next?

'Please get your people to make a tent for me,' says God. 'I'd like to come and live among them' (25:8–9).

What is this? The God who has come down in fire and cloud to the top of the mountain wants to come right on down to the bottom of the mountain and dwell in the midst of his people . . . in a tent, just like them! (Well, OK, just a bit more special than theirs, but the whole thing is simple enough to be transportable on six ox-carts, as in Numbers 7:1–9.) *God wants to go camping with his people!* In fact, God says this is what he's been wanting to do all along. That great liberation from slavery, that giving of the Ten Commandments, that sealing of the covenant – for God, those were stepping stones to *this* moment: himself dwelling in the midst of his own people. This is where the God of heaven will dwell with his people on earth. For the time being, this will be God's local address on earth.

So God *comes down*. God *moves in*. Advent in a tent.

God says this was his purpose in bringing Israel out of Egypt. When everything will be constructed and ready:

> Then I will dwell among the Israelites and be their God. They will know that I am the LORD their God, *who brought them out of Egypt so that I might dwell among them*. I am the LORD their God.
> (29:45–46)

That's a powerful statement of God's intentions, very similar to 6:6–7. From now on, Israel would *know* Yahweh their God *both* as the One who had redeemed them out of slavery in Egypt (historical fact) *and* as the One who dwelt in their midst (ongoing experience).

And isn't that the way it is for us too? We know the Lord Jesus *both* as the One who died and rose again for our redemption (historical fact) *and* as the One who dwells in our hearts through his Spirit (ongoing experience).

So in this tabernacle advent, God came down from heavenly glory to dwell in an earthly tent. Surely, there is something incarnational about this, inspiring John to write, 'The Word became flesh and made his dwelling [the word means 'pitched his tent' or 'tabernacled'] among us. We have seen his glory . . .' (John 1:14). The Creator of heaven and earth came down to make an earthly tent his dwelling place at Sinai. And now the same invisible God has 'pitched his tent' in the flesh of the man Jesus. The man-made tabernacle becomes the metaphor for God-made-man. Jesus becomes the 'place' where heaven and earth truly meet, where God and humanity are reconciled, where sacrificial atonement is accomplished once and for all.

The tabernacle was, of course, eventually replaced by the temple. So Paul uses temple imagery to express the transformation accomplished by the gospel. The new humanity of believing Jews and Gentiles united together becomes God's home on earth: 'In him you too are being built together to become a dwelling in which God lives by his Spirit' (Ephesians 2:22). A stupendous reality that we can only grasp in prayer and faith – which is what Paul does indeed pray for.

Make his prayer your prayer today, and rejoice that Christ dwells in you.

A prayer

I pray that out of his glorious riches he may strengthen you with power through his Spirit in your inner being, so that Christ may dwell in your hearts through faith. And I pray that you, being rooted and established in love, may have power, together with all the Lord's holy people, to grasp how wide and long and high and deep is the love of Christ, and to know this love that surpasses knowledge – that you may be filled to the measure of all the fullness of God.

(Ephesians 3:16–19)

13

God comes to forgive

Bible reading: Exodus 32:1–14; 33:18 – 34:9

From John Stott:

> Sin has been described in terms of 'getting rid of the Lord God' in order to put ourselves in his place in a haughty spirit of 'God-almightiness'.
> (TCOC, p. 107)

> The essential background to the cross is a balanced understanding of the gravity of sin and the majesty of God. If we diminish either, we thereby diminish the cross. If we re-interpret sin as a lapse instead of a rebellion, and God as indulgent instead of indignant, then naturally the cross appears superfluous. But to dethrone God and enthrone ourselves not only dispenses with the cross; it also degrades both God and man.
> (TCOC, p. 110)

*

'Let's play "Mummy's coming"!'

It was a game our children invented, which they only told us about later when they thought it was probably safe to do so. They'd go into the lounge and do all the things they had been explicitly instructed *not* to do, like jumping up and down on the sofa, throwing the cushions ... until one would shout, 'Mummy's coming!' Whereupon they'd sit down, silent and motionless, and the last one down was 'out'. Mummy's advent – even imaginary – would spell judgment or joy, depending on what she found when she opened the door.

What will God find when he looks down the mountain – or, worse still, comes down in person? What if the cry goes up, 'God's coming!'?

Don't you feel a massive shock when you come to Exodus 32? For seven chapters we have been in the glorious presence of God with Moses on the mountain top, visualizing the sumptuous beauty, the intricacies of white, blue and scarlet embroidery, the glinting of gold and silver and bronze, the warm glow of oil lamps, and fragrance of incense, that were to adorn the planned place of divine dwelling.

But in six verses we are horrified at the blatant disobedience and dissolute idolatry with a ridiculous bovine god-substitute. Aaron and the people break the first three commandments, by explicitly rejecting the God who had brought them up out of Egypt (20:2–3; 32:4); by fashioning an idol; and by using the name of Yahweh in a blasphemous parody of the covenant ceremony of chapter 24 (32:5–6; 24:5, 11).

One scholar commented that for Israel to behave like this so soon after their repeated vows and the covenant meal of chapter 24 is like committing adultery on your wedding night.

So, in his first advent in these suspense-filled chapters (32 – 34), God threatens to destroy the whole people totally. It will be the end of 'the children of Israel', replaced by 'the children of Moses' (32:10). But that idea is unthinkable to Moses. He steps into the gap and boldly tells God that the idea has to be unthinkable for God too (32:11–13). 'Think about what you have just done for these people, Lord. Think about the reputation of your own name in the region. Think about your promise to Abraham. Think again!' Those points touch God's heart and he responds by withholding his threatened destruction – though not without a measure of vocal anger and graphic punishment filling the rest of the chapter.

The suspense thickens as we agonize our way through the intense interactions between Moses and Aaron, Moses and the people, and

Moses and God – all against a background of pain and mourning (33:4–6). Through it all, Moses is determined not only that God should *not* utterly destroy the people, but rather that God should 'carry' their wrongdoing (that is the basic meaning of the Hebrew word translated 'forgive'), and that he would keep his original intention to go with them, leading them and dwelling among them. And if God would not do these things, well then, God might as well forget the tabernacle, forget Israel's distinctiveness, forget Moses too, forget God's plans for the nations. God gets the point and agrees. God's presence will go with them (33:12–17). Phew!

I think that would have been enough for me. But Moses hasn't finished. 'Now show me your glory,' he says (verse 18). Hadn't he had enough of the glory of God up the mountain for the past month? Moses wants an even more intimate understanding of his God. And that leads to the second advent in these chapters, the one in which God comes down (34:5) to a conveniently nearby mountain crag (33:21–22), to proclaim the essence and depths of his character – to declare the God he truly is.

To see or not to see, that may be the question (verses 19–23 are mysterious), but what matters is what Moses *heard God say*. Moses had asked to see God's *glory*, and God says he will cause all his *goodness* to pass in front of Moses (just try to imagine that!). God's glory is God's goodness. Or God's goodness is his glory. Either way round, it rings the joy bells of heaven and earth and the whole Bible.

Who then is this good and glorious God? He tells us himself:

The LORD, the LORD, the compassionate and gracious God, slow to anger, abounding in love and faithfulness, maintaining love to thousands, and forgiving [carrying] wickedness, rebellion and sin. Yet he does not leave the guilty unpunished. (34:6–7)

Please read those words aloud and repeat after me, 'This is "the Old Testament God".' For it is sad that so many people (including many Christians who ought to know better) still imagine the so-called 'Old Testament God' as a God of unrelieved violence and impetuous

59

anger, whereas God emphatically self-identifies here as the God of compassion and grace, and slow to anger.

Now, we cannot omit that last line of verse 7. God does not leave wickedness unpunished – as the Israelites had just experienced. The tension between that line and the previous ones (how do forgiveness and punishment go together?) runs through the Old Testament. Yahweh is the God who punishes *and* the God who forgives. Yahweh is the God of wrath *and* the God of compassion.

It's a tension resolved only at the cross of Christ, where both truths about God are ultimately united. For indeed, God finally did not leave the guilty unpunished, but chose to bear the consequences of sin and guilt in God's own self, in his own Son. There on the cross God demonstrated in flesh and blood all that he had declared about himself as Yahweh, God of Israel, the compassionate and gracious God, carrying sin and abounding in love.

How we still need Moses' final plea to God in verse 9! Forgiven sinners are sinners still, and stiff-necked ones at that. God will have a lot more 'carrying' to do with this people – and with us – until the journey's over and we sin no more.

An exercise
In case we think Exodus 34:6–7 is merely a one-off Advent special for a close friend of God, its phrases are threaded through the rest of the Old Testament in many places, and explode in the kaleidoscopic riot of God's redeeming grace, mercy, love, faithfulness and forgiveness in the New Testament. Trace them through these passages: Numbers 14:18; Nehemiah 9:17; Psalms 78:38; 86:5, 15; 99:8; 103:8; 145:8–9; Joel 2:13; Jonah 4:2; Micah 7:18–19.

14

God comes to lead the way

Bible reading: Exodus 40:17–38

[John Stott] looks back with gratitude to the gracious pursuit of the hound of heaven down the arches of the years.
(IS, p. 282)

Paul's mind [in Romans 8:28–39] now sweeps over the whole plan and purpose of God from a past eternity to an eternity still to come, from the divine foreknowledge and predestination to the divine love from which absolutely nothing will ever be able to separate us . . .

So the burden of Paul's climax is the eternal security of God's people, on account of the unchangeability of God's purpose, which is itself due to the eternal steadfastness of God's love.
(John Stott, BST, *Romans*, p. 246)

*

He didn't bring us this far to leave us
He didn't teach us to swim to let us drown
He didn't build His home in us to move away
He didn't lift us up to let us down.

This old song appealed to me, as we sat around of an evening in Pune, India, in the 1980s, with coffee and guitars, on cushions and mats in our apartment, with some of the students from Union Biblical Seminary. For, in spite of its curious mixture of metaphors, the song does capture some precious biblical truths that meant a lot to those young Indian sisters and brothers. The God who had invested so much in their salvation, in protecting them on their varied journeys and battles of faith and witness, and in getting them to seminary to train for a lifetime of service – this same God would see them through, would never fail or forsake them. Whatever lay ahead, they could trust God to lead the way and travel with them.

Most of them were in their twenties. My wife and I have met some of them over the years, and, now in their fifties, they would sing the same song still, having proved its truth through many struggles and some harrowing times of suffering. They have walked with God, and God has walked with them.

Two of the images in the song reflect our final reading in Exodus today: God making his home in his people, and God accompanying his people on their journey.

First comes a summary of the second half of the whole book (verses 17–33). Moses sets up the tabernacle in full compliance with God's instructions. With an echo of God's work in creation, Moses *finished* the work (40:33), and *blessed* the people (39:43). Then comes an advent of astonishing speed (40:34–35). The cloud and the glory demonstrate the visible, almost tangible, presence of God. They signify beyond doubt that God himself has come. Here their arrival is emphatically mentioned twice. God has moved in.

In the Hebrew text, there is no break between verses 33 and 34. We could easily translate, '*No sooner* had Moses finished the work than the cloud covered the tent of meeting, and the glory of the LORD filled the tabernacle.' It's as if God couldn't wait to move into the home he had ordered, couldn't wait to be where he had wanted to be all along – right in the midst of his people.

So God comes to take up residence in an earthly tent, knowing of course (as we do too, having read the rest of the story) that this tabernacle advent at Mount Sinai is but the foreshadowing in linen, goat-hair and leather of three other definitive advent moments in the drama of Scripture: Bethlehem, Pentecost and the return of Christ.

- God came to tabernacle among us in the flesh of the incarnate Son (as we considered three days ago).
- God came in the outpouring of his Spirit to dwell in the temple that is his church and to make his home in the hearts of all believers in Jesus, whose bodies (says Paul, in remarkable imagery) are temples of the Holy Spirit.
- The day will come when the glory of God will fill the city of God (which needs no temple), and all creation will hear the same voice that once spoke at Sinai, saying, 'Look! God's dwelling-place is now among the people, and he will dwell with them. They will be his people, and God himself will be with them and be their God' (Revelation 21:3).

Aren't those three great biblical moments enough to set your heart rejoicing as we come to the end of this week of Advent?

The second image in the song is how God accompanies us on our journey. Exodus ends with a forward look. The people must move on from Mount Sinai – the Promised Land awaits. A long journey lies ahead for Israel, and an even longer one for God's people in the whole Bible story to follow. Yesterday we heard Moses pleading for God to go with his people. But as the people follow the leading of the cloud of God's presence (verses 36–38), we realize that it is not so much a case of God going with the people as the people going with God.

This closing image of Exodus – Israel on the move with God – reminds us of that powerful biblical metaphor of the way, the journey, the pilgrimage. It applies not only to our personal life journeys, but to the whole people of God through history and in every generation. It's a journey in which we participate in the mission of God. Like Israel, we owe our existence to God's redeeming grace. Like Israel, we are summoned to live for God's glory, and for the blessing of the nations in fulfilment of his promise to Abraham.

Is that how you see what it means to walk with God, and for God to walk with you?

A reflection

Like Israel, we are a sinful and stiff-necked people. But, like them, we step forward with the promise of God behind us and the mission of God before us. We journey in humility, depending utterly on the grace and forgiveness of God in Christ. We journey with the presence of God in our midst and in our hearts, to guide, protect and sustain us until the journey is done, God's mission is accomplished, and the last trumpet sounds the final advent. Until then, as the Lord said on another mountain, echoing what he first said to Moses, 'I am with you always, to the very end of the age' (Matthew 28:20).

Week 3

THE GOD WHO CAME AS PROMISED

'*Maranatha*! Come, Lord Jesus!' we pray.

We long for the second advent of our Lord and Saviour. And why? Surely because of the terrible mess our world is in. The overwhelming tide of wickedness and suffering, of international tensions, along with the seeming acceleration of natural disasters and the extremes of global climate breakdown, make us long more and more for Christ to come and put things right. As we sing in Lewis Hensley's hymn (1864),

> Thy kingdom come, O God,
> thy rule, O Christ, begin;
> break with thine iron rod
> the tyrannies of sin.

But how can we be sure that Christ will come again, and come to reign? Because of the historical facts of his first coming, and the unambiguous promise of God: 'This same Jesus, who has been taken from you into heaven, will come back in the same way you have seen him go into heaven' (Acts 1:11). In other words, we ground our hope for what God will do in the future on our knowledge of what he has done in the past.

It was exactly the same for Old Testament Israel. We saw last week in the book of Exodus how that great event became the foundation of Israel's faith and expectations from God for ever after. If God could do *that* (and he did), then God can surely do *this* (whatever the need might be, in personal or national life). As the centuries went by, the prophets of Israel began to look forward to a climactic moment of future salvation for which only exodus language was adequate. There would be a *new* exodus, a *new* defeat of God's enemies, a *new* deliverance, a *new* way through the wilderness.

So, when God came again in the person of the incarnate Son of God, it was the fulfilment of a wide range of scriptural promises. We shall sample just a few of those this week, to illustrate our subtitle: *Advent in All the Scriptures*. God's coming, whether as a past fact to be celebrated or as a future event to be expected, is woven through the whole Bible.

First of all, however, we begin the week of devotions again with a psalm, in which David remembers how God has given him a desperately needed personal 'exodus'. He then turns that experience into testimony and challenge, and finally longs for God to come and do the same again. He had waited before and been answered, but now he is waiting again.

A prayer for week 3 of Advent

Almighty God, who sent your servant John the Baptist to prepare your people for the coming of your Son, inspire us, the ministers and stewards of your truth, to turn our disobedient hearts to the law of love, that when he comes again in glory, we may stand with confidence before him as our Judge, who is alive and reigns with you and the Holy Spirit, one God, now and for ever.

15

Waiting for God

Bible reading: Psalm 40

No sooner had we entered a shop than John [Stott] seemed
to want to leave ... browsing was certainly not one of his
enjoyments.
(Matthew Smith, JS: APBHF, p. 202)

The psalmist was down a slimy pit, full of mud and mire ... In
his helplessness, unable himself to climb out, he waited
patiently for the LORD, and the following verses emphasise,
stage by stage, the mighty deliverance of God who first heard
his cry, then stooped down and drew him out of the mud, then
set his feet securely upon rock, and finally put a fresh song of
praise in his mouth, leading many to believe (verses 1–3) ...
   But God in grace does more even than this. If He has written
His law in a book that we may know it, and whispered it into
our ears that we may understand it, He also inscribes it in our
hearts so that we 'delight to do it' (verse 8, RSV) ... knowing,
loving and doing God's will, which is partially true of all His
children, found its perfect fulfilment in His incarnate Son.
(John Stott, FP, pp. 50–52)

*

'Wait in line!' is how our American friends express the more polite
British 'Form an orderly queue, please'. I hear those words in
American airports, and how I hate them! I hate waiting in gen-
eral ... waiting around, wasting time, getting nothing done. So
frustrating. Patience is one part of the fruit of the Spirit that seems
to struggle to grow in my life. Just ask my wife ...

There is a great deal of waiting for God in the Bible, however, and Advent is a good time to be reminded of it. Abraham and Sarah waited a quarter of a century for Isaac. The Israelites waited several centuries in Egypt. And they waited another whole generation in the wilderness (their own fault). The exiles of Judah waited two generations for God to return with them to their land. Then God's people waited several more centuries before the coming of the Messiah. I think that puts my own small and impatient frustrations in a humbling perspective.

But here's the thing: in every case, *God came in the end*. God delivered what he had promised. You might have to wait, but God can be trusted. That is the assurance that guarantees ultimate vindication for the martyrs of Jesus Christ, who are told to 'wait a little longer' until the full number of their fellow believers will have been slain (Revelation 6:9–11).

I wonder if you can identify with the following. There was a period in my life that went on for years when it seemed that God would not answer my prayer. Or, to be more precise, God sometimes beautifully answered my prayers for others, but seemed deaf to my prayer for myself regarding a particularly distressing issue. In the end he did answer, and the waiting and longing came to an end. Although nothing as severe has happened since, I trust that if it ever should, I will be fortified in my faith and hope by that previous experience of waiting for God.

David's waiting in Psalm 40 is both past and present. It is actually a very balanced psalm: it begins and ends in desperate trouble and agonized waiting (verses 1, 17). But because he knows that God heard and saved him, after his first experience of patient waiting, he can confidently ask God to do the same now – even if his last words are a touching human plea that he won't have to wait quite so long this time – 'do not delay!'

David's psalm is balanced in other ways too. Can you spot some of the matching themes in each half? This means that the key message comes right in the middle, in verses 6–8. And it is a challenge.

When God comes to hear our prayer at last and deliver us, what should be our response? For David, God had come to him, so he needed to come to God: 'Here I am, I have come,' he says (verse 7). One good advent deserves another. But David knew that he needed to come to God not merely with the worship of his lips, or even with the standard sacrifices that constituted the normal worship of his people. No, what God wanted was the listening of his ears, the commitment of his heart, and the obedience of his life. Or, as Paul will later call it, 'the obedience of faith' (Romans 1:5; 16:26, ESV).

Now we know that David did not live up to that desire (sincere as it was in this psalm) in his actual life, with tragic results. But for 'great David's greater Son', these verses express not just a commitment, but a reality. Jesus came to do God's will, to listen to his Father's voice and to be obedient even unto death, as Hebrews perceived (Hebrews 10:5–10). His is the example we are to follow, with the help of the Holy Spirit.

Meanwhile, Advent calls us to come to God, even as we wait, with hope, patience and joy, for him to come to us. There can be rejoicing even in waiting, as Habakkuk shows (Habakkuk 3:17–18).

An affirmation and a prayer
> We wait in hope for the LORD;
>> he is our help and our shield.
> In him our hearts rejoice,
>> for we trust in his holy name.
> May your unfailing love be with us, LORD,
>> even as we put our hope in you.
> (Psalm 33:20–22)

16

Running with good news

Bible reading: Isaiah 52:7–10

From John Stott:

> Mission is an unavoidable deduction from the universal
> lordship of Jesus Christ.
> (TG, TCC series, p. 75)

> The need for heralds is now confirmed from Scripture: *As
> it is written, 'how beautiful are the feet of those who bring
> good news!'* If those who proclaimed the good news of release
> from Babylonian exile were thus celebrated, how much more
> welcome the heralds of the gospel of Christ should be! . . .
> Christ sends heralds; heralds preach; people hear; hearers
> believe; believers call; and those who call are saved.
> (BST, *Romans*, p. 286)

*

Do you remember the film *Chariots of Fire*? In the mesmerizing
opening sequence, with its throbbing theme music, all we see are
feet running along the edge of the sea at St Andrews, Scotland –
running feet of the 1924 Olympic athletes in training.

The poet-prophet of our text today calls on our imagination. We
are in the ruins of Jerusalem, anxiously gazing out to the east from
the rubble of the walls. At least two generations have passed since
Nebuchadnezzar destroyed the city and took the people into exile
in Babylon (it happened in 587 BC). Will they ever come back? Will
God ever come back (for he too had departed from his temple and
city)? Suddenly (verse 7) we see the running feet of a single

messenger, loping breathlessly across the eastern hills towards the city, bringing (we desperately hope) good news.

And it is! 'It's *peace!*' he gasps. 'It's *good*. We're *saved!*', and with a triumphant shout, '*The* LORD, *your God is King!*'

This was the good news that the exiles longed to hear. Yet again God has won the victory over his enemies and is coming to deliver his people. When God comes, he comes to *reign*. And when God reigns, it will mean *peace*. Life will be *good* (as creation was in the beginning), and they will be *saved* (liberated from exile).

That message of a single runner is then amplified by a 'chorus' of watchmen – the imaginary sentries on Jerusalem's broken walls. For they can see, behind the messenger, the Lord God himself coming back (verse 8). The God who *reigns* is the God who *returns* (as he had said he would, 40:9–11)!

That news brings even the rubble of Jerusalem to life in joyful songs (verse 9), exodus songs, for God has *redeemed* his people once more, liberating them from bondage, bringing comfort to those who had suffered long (40:1–2).

The crescendo of rejoicing increases as the prophet opens up his vision to a future horizon far beyond just the return from exile – to God's salvation extending to *all nations* and *the ends of the earth* (verse 10). Can you hear those echoes of Abraham again?

But how will God accomplish this global mission of salvation? By his *holy arm* (verse 10). Baring the arm portrays God like a soldier throwing off his heavy cloak ready for victory in battle. We've met 'the arm of the LORD' before. It lifts, carries and cuddles the struggling lambs among God's people (40:10–11). It brings salvation and justice to the nations (51:5). But above all, it (or rather he) will be the Servant of the Lord who will suffer and die for us (53:1–6).

Here then is the gospel. This is the good news that is for the exiles of Judah and also for the ends of the earth, to bring joy and comfort to all nations. It is the advent of the God who *reigns* (verse 7), who *returns* (verse 8) and who *redeems* the whole world (verses 9–10) through his mighty arm, stretched out in victorious battle, in gentle compassion and in suffering love. Rejoice! The Lord is King!

'Go, tell it on the mountain, that Jesus Christ is born.' Will you be singing that song this Christmas? It is most likely inspired by Isaiah 40:9 and 52:7. For indeed, our text, which originally brought hope to the exiles, has a gospel horizon. This text lands in Bethlehem, moves to Galilee and then to Calvary.

Jesus was, and is, God reigning. He preached that God's kingdom had come, in and through himself. But it had come like seed growing, or yeast rising – at work in the world in hidden ways through those in whose lives God reigns, lives committed to Christ's lordship (Matthew 28:18–20), lives seeking first God's kingdom and justice, lives going out into the world under the sovereign governance of the crucified and risen Lamb on the throne of God.

That is our mission. Are you working for it?

Jesus was, and is, God returning. God had promised that he would return to his temple, sending a messenger (Elijah) before his face (Malachi 3:1; 4:5). And, in fulfilment of the vision of Zechariah 9:9, Jesus rode a donkey into Jerusalem and went straight to the temple – the Lord returning to Zion. And the same Lord Jesus will return again . . .

That is our glorious hope. Are you living for it?

Jesus was, and is, God redeeming. So, finally, Jesus went to Jerusalem, and the arm of the Lord was stretched out on the cross for the redemption of the world. Christmas was God rolling up his sleeves for Calvary.

That is our salvation. Are you rejoicing in it?

This Advent, let's heartily reaffirm these great biblical truths. They bring enormous hope in the midst of a world sadly still full of injustice and oppression, of exiles and displaced peoples, of waste places and ruins, of sheer mountains of suffering of humanity and creation. Advent hope: God is coming back and will put all things right. That is the ultimate horizon of our text. It finally lands in acts 6 and 7 of the drama of Scripture (flick back to the diagram on p. 2). That's what it means to me.

A challenge (to myself)

'But what does it mean to *them*?' I asked myself as I walked along Tottenham Court Road, near my house, thinking about this text. What does it mean to the crowds on the street that Jesus is the reigning Lord of history, the returning King of creation, and the Redeemer and Saviour of the world? And the answer seemed to bounce off the buildings: 'Nothing at all. How can it mean anything, if nobody has ever told them?' And then this text also seemed to bounce off the walls, in the form that Paul quoted it:

> How, then, can they call on the one they have not believed in? And how can they believe in the one of whom they have not heard? And how can they hear without someone preaching to them? And how can anyone preach unless they are sent? As it is written: 'How beautiful are the feet of those who bring good news!'
>
> (Romans 10:14–15)

The only things that make feet 'beautiful' are the running shoes of the gospel. Let's get them on today.

17

A Ruler from Bethlehem – of all places!

Bible reading: Micah 5:1–5

From John Stott:

> He was nothing much to look at, and certainly no ambassador for muscular Christianity. Yet as he spoke, I was riveted.
> Description of E. J. H. Nash (Bash), youth camp leader
> (JS: TMOAL, p. 93)

> It is especially remarkable that Matthew, the most Jewish of the four evangelists, nevertheless portrays near the beginning of his Gospel the visit of those mysterious Magi [wise men], representatives of the Gentile nations, and at its end the commission of the risen Lord to go and disciple the nations. Thus his kingdom community would grow like a mustard seed from tiny, unpropitious beginnings until it fills the whole earth.
> (TIC, p. 26)

*

Can you imagine what it must be like to live in a besieged city? We've seen the horrors of siege warfare: in Syria, Iraq, Yemen . . . the enemy all around, missiles coming in, water and food running out, no medical supplies, starvation, epidemics, death, fear, anger, no way out, despair. That's where our reading begins (verse 1) and ends (verse 5).

Assyria! – that aggressive empire, brutal, vicious, violent. Twenty years ago they smashed the northern kingdom of Israel. Now

Assyria is right on Judah's doorstep, in our faces, mocking and threatening our own king! What possible hope can there be? Judah needs a new leader. Is there a Gideon or a Deborah in the house? Where are the troops (verse 1)?

God calmly answers, 'Don't panic, I've got it all under control. I've got a ruler all lined up.' But where? 'In Bethlehem' (verse 2a). Where did you say? Bethlehem was a tiny village, so insignificant (even if it had been the birthplace of David) that you had to give the name of somewhere larger nearby to help people even grasp where it was – Ephrathah (a bit like our old address: Easneye, *Near Ware*, Hertfordshire).

But that's partly the point. So often in the Bible, God goes for the smallest and least to achieve his purpose. Gideon, Saul, David – all said they were 'the least' in their families. Mary even turned this into a song – God puts down the proud and lifts up the humble and weak. Paul turns it into a principle: God does not choose the proud, the wealthy, the powerful, but the lowly and least in society, like the believers in Corinth.

Don't you think this in itself is encouraging? Maybe you sometimes feel very small – a tiny cog in a big company, just one of many in your workplace, or simply the pressure of a pagan and arrogant culture. When you're tempted to feel like that, remember Bethlehem – smallest village in Judah!

So who is this ruler from Bethlehem going to be? He will be *for* God and *from* God (verse 2b). God says, 'out of you [Bethlehem] will come a ruler *for me*' – not, as you might expect, 'a ruler *for you*, Judah'. Surely they were the ones who needed it! This ruler, unlike their present kings, will rule on God's behalf, doing God's will and fulfilling God's purpose. And he will also come *from God*. The words 'from of old, from ancient times' could just mean that he will be a descendant of David (already some 400 years ago). But more probably, Micah means that this ruler will have his roots, his origin, *in God himself* (Deuteronomy 33:27).

How wonderfully hopeful! Here comes One who in some sense embodies the ancient identity and power of the God of Israel. God has found a Ruler for us, and he's on his way! Hooray!

But not yet! Uh-oh. He will come only after a long time in which Israel will feel abandoned by God, until a mother will give birth to a son (verse 3). But right now, how can such a mysterious long-term prophecy help the besieged city? We wait to see.

First, we are told what this future coming Ruler will accomplish (verses 3–5). The language is mysterious, but several themes are clear:

- He will bring unity to God's divided people (verse 3b).
- He will be the great shepherd (king) of God's flock (verse 4a).
- His rule will be an embodiment of the reign of God.
- He will bring an end to violence and fear, for people will dwell in peace and security.
- And, climactically, he will extend this reign of unity, authority and security 'to the ends of the earth' (verses 4b–5a; I hope you're getting used to hearing these echoes of Abraham!).

So *he will be our peace*, the Prince of Peace, as Isaiah calls him (Isaiah 9:6). How wonderful!

But wait! What help is this to our besieged city? Telling us that God's Ruler will come, but only at some distant future time? Well, if the Ruler to come in the future is actually 'from of old', then he shares the identity of Yahweh, the age-old God of Israel. So the One who will come in the *future* is the One who will deliver Jerusalem *now* – and defeat the power of Assyria. And that is indeed what would happen in the great deliverance of Jerusalem from Sennacherib in 701 BC.

That is Micah's vision of a mysterious paradoxical future. God's Ruler will come from an insignificant nowhere town, Bethlehem, yet he will reign to the ends of the earth. Which takes us, of course, from Micah to Matthew and the Magi (Matthew 2:1–12). Matthew sees Micah's vision fulfilled in a humble house in little Bethlehem, in a toddler less than two years old, and in a world that was just as violent and oppressive as in Micah's day (and still is).

One day, some strange men turned up in Bethlehem: Magi, possibly astrologers from Mesopotamia, bringing their gifts and worship. God had revealed himself through the stars, and then more clearly through the scriptures of Micah's prophecy, which led them to Bethlehem and to a little boy called Jesus.

Here then is God's Ruler, Matthew is telling us, through this story and his quotation from Micah. Here is the One born to be the Messiah and King, born as Micah said in the most insignificant little village in Judah (but not so any longer), yet born to rule to the ends of the earth.

That is the gospel horizon of our text. For this boy of Bethlehem will be the crucified Man of Calvary thirty years later. And then he will rise again! And in his risen victorious life he will declare, 'All authority in heaven and on earth has been given to me' (Matthew 28:18).

Just as Micah said, 'his greatness will reach to the ends of the earth'. That's a vision that is well on its way to fulfilment through the mission of God's people through the ages.

O little town of Bethlehem
How still we see thee lie.
Above thy deep and dreamless sleep
The silent stars go by.
Yet in thy dark streets shineth
The everlasting light
The hopes and fears of all the years
Are met in thee tonight.[1]

---

1   Phillips Brooks, 1868.

18

God is on his way!
Get ready and repent

Bible reading: Luke 1:57–80

From John Stott:

> Nobody is free who is unforgiven. If I were not sure of God's
> forgiveness, I could not look you in the face, and I certainly
> could not look God in the face.
> (WIAAC, p. 88)

> Convicted of sin and conscience-stricken, Peter's hearers [on
> the day of Pentecost] asked anxiously what they should do
> (Acts 2:37). Peter replied that they must repent, completely
> changing their mind about Jesus and their attitude to him,
> and be baptised in his name, submitting to the humiliation
> of baptism, which Jews regarded as necessary for Gentile
> converts only, and submitting to it in the name of the very
> person they had previously rejected. This would be a clear
> public token of their repentance – and of their faith in him.
> (BST, *Acts*, p. 78)

*

I wonder if Peter had been among those who went to the Jordan to
be baptized by John the Baptist? Very likely, don't you think? That
would explain why he was prepared to follow Jesus immediately.

Well, now Jesus' earthly life was over, and Peter had learned how
to preach, like John: 'Repent and be baptized!' But we need to go
back to the beginning, for Luke shows us that the coming of John

had been a kind of 'advent' in itself, a fulfilment of God's great promises in Scripture.

Zechariah and Elizabeth, John's parents, were sincere Israelite believers (Luke 1:6). They knew their Scriptures intimately – especially the Psalms. So, when Zechariah bursts into prophetic speech, it is basically a psalm of praise: 'Blessed be the Lord, the God of Israel!' (Psalms 41:13; 72:18; 106:48). Israel had sung words like these whenever God had come to their rescue.

But this is the big one. God is coming to fulfil all those great scriptural promises – especially the ones to Abraham and David. God is coming to give his people deliverance from their enemies; to show mercy in the midst of judgment; to restore them to freedom from oppression and attack; and to enable them to live without fear and in peace in their own land, and serve God in holy and righteous living (verses 69–75).

Quite a catalogue! That's what they longed for. And Zechariah says, 'It's here!' God is coming to visit again! And he's coming to bring salvation – not just from our enemies (verse 71), but from our sins (verse 77). Zechariah probably didn't yet know the name of Mary's soon-to-be-born son, but he certainly expresses its meaning.

Eventually Zechariah gets to the point: the big question that all his family and friends were asking on this special day (verse 66). 'What will *this* child be – if he isn't going to have his father's name and be a priest like him?' So Zechariah tells the world what the angel Gabriel had told him (check 1:16–17), which he must have told Elizabeth (by writing it down, I suppose), how his name was to be John (verses 60, 63; which means 'The Lord is gracious').

Zechariah turns to the one-week-old baby in his old hands and says, 'You, my child, will be called a prophet of the Most High.' Well, that was true of all the prophets. But not this extra bit: 'You will go on before the Lord to prepare the way for him' (verse 76). That rings some bells, and two prophecies in particular. 'A voice of one calling: "In the wilderness prepare the way for the LORD"' (Isaiah 40:3), and 'I will send my messenger, who will prepare the way before me . . . See, I will send the prophet Elijah to you before that great and dreadful day of the LORD comes' (Malachi 3:1; 4:5).

God is on his way! But the divine Visitor is sending his calling card in advance. John will be the messenger of the Lord; he will be the 'Elijah' promised by Malachi.

Now one thing we know about Elijah is that he was a great preacher of repentance. He called the people to make their minds up and turn back to Yahweh their God. So John will be that kind of preacher-prophet too. Why? Because God is coming! And before God comes, things have got to change. Luke's record of John's preaching shows exactly that strong emphasis on repentance which would be demonstrated in changed lives (Luke 1:1–14).

You might like to think of Advent as a 'John the Baptist season'. It is a time of expectation and preparation, as we look forward to celebrating Christ's first coming and anticipate his second.

What should it mean for us, to be a people *prepared for the Lord*?

Zechariah offers us a clue in verses 74–75, and it is very down-to-earth and practical. Why did God redeem his people out of Egypt? Not just so they could go to heaven when they died, but rather, 'Let my people go *that they may serve me*' (Exodus 4:23). So it is for us today. Our salvation is not an insurance plan in the face of death, or an exit strategy from a doomed planet. God saved us in order 'to enable us *to serve him without fear, in holiness and righteousness before him all our days*'.

Isn't that the opposite of some popular perceptions of being a Christian, which are more like: 'to enable God to serve me without inconvenience . . .'? What will it mean for you this week, this Advent, and when you go back to work or routines after Christmas and New Year, to be *serving God*? And to do so in 'holiness' (which means in a way that is distinctive from the world around), and in 'righteousness' (which means a life of integrity, honesty and seeking justice). We are servants, and the Master is returning. Let's be doing what we were told (Luke 12:43).

This first chapter of Luke's Gospel simply throbs with joy: angel announcements; surprise pregnancies and joyful births; good news of salvation to come; and sunrise for those living in the shadow of death. Zechariah is bursting with the joy of knowing that God is coming, because God is keeping his promise and fulfilling his plan.

Advent is a celebration of the *faithfulness* of God, so foundational for our hope for the future. God has made his plan known to us, and he will accomplish it. Always has, always will. And we rightly rejoice in that.

But Luke also knew what God's plan would mean both for John and Jesus. The salvation, forgiveness and tender mercy of our God (verses 77–78) would certainly and joyfully come – but at great cost. Both the messenger of God and the Messiah of God were executed, obedient unto death. One ended up with his head on a plate; the other with his hands and feet nailed to a cross. John suffered under Herod the tetrarch. Jesus 'suffered under Pontius Pilate'. And Jesus rose again . . . 'according to the Scriptures' (1 Corinthians 15:1–4).

Hallelujah! No wonder we rejoice.

An Advent affirmation to help us rejoice
Christ has died. Christ is risen. Christ will come again.

19

Are you the One who is to come?

Bible readings: Matthew 11:2–6; Isaiah 35

From John Stott:

> Deluded people delude nobody but themselves ... Jesus has succeeded in persuading (or deluding) millions of people, for the very good reason that he seems to be what he claimed to be. There is no dichotomy between his character and his claims. (WIAAC, p. 45)

> The most striking feature of the teaching of Jesus is that he was constantly talking about himself ... The great question to which the first phase of his teaching leads is, 'Who do you say that I am?' He refers back to figures from the distant past and makes the astonishing claim that Abraham rejoiced to see his day, that Moses wrote about him, that the Scriptures point to him, and that indeed in the three great divisions of the Old Testament – the Law, the Prophets and the Writings – there are things 'concerning himself'.
> (BC, pp. 33–35)

*

What happens to your faith when you are imprisoned for it?

What happened to John the Baptist when Herod threw him in prison? He had told people to be ready for the coming of God's

Messiah (Matthew 3:11). Indeed, John's own birth had been a significant advent in itself. 'There was a man sent from God whose name was John. He came as a witness to testify concerning that light, so that through him all might believe' (John 1:6–7).

But, in prison, did John's belief that Jesus of Nazareth truly was the Messiah begin to falter, in spite of what people were telling him (Matthew 11:2–3)? After all, if Jesus really was the Messiah, why hadn't he arranged a miraculous deliverance? Or did John send his own disciples to Jesus in order to help *them* to believe for themselves? Hard to know.

When I was a teenager, Richard Wurmbrand stayed briefly in our home in Northern Ireland. He was a pastor from Romania who had been imprisoned and tortured, along with many others, by communist state authorities, in those years before the fall of the Iron Curtain. He had spent years in solitary confinement. His books became famous, including the one we had all read, *Tortured for Christ*. Pastor Wurmbrand's faith survived, but not without great testing, and times of doubt and struggle.

He recounted an experience of sensing Satan's presence with him in his cell. 'He was very near. He laughed at me. He said, "Where's Jesus? Why doesn't he save you, and the others who believed in him? He's a false Messiah!"'

Did John have similar moments?

Here is Jesus facing John's disciples and their question: 'Are you really the one who is to come, or should we expect someone else?' How will Jesus respond? Will he flash a shiny photo ID card: 'Jesus of Nazareth, The *Real* Messiah'? Will there be a glowing halo round his head silently rebuking their impudence: 'Can't you see that I am God?' No, he simply invites them to look around and see what is happening. He points to the whole range of his healing and restoring and preaching work

But (typical Jesus!) he does so with the very strong echo of a great prophetic scripture. Jesus' words in Matthew 11:5 are not quite a direct quote of Isaiah 35:5–6, but close enough so that there is no doubt that's what Jesus has in mind – his listeners would instantly recognize them. Jesus uses Scripture to make very clear who he is and what his actions mean. No, my friends, you don't need to look for anybody else. Jesus *is* the one whose coming the Scriptures promised. You can reassure John of that!

Look more closely at Isaiah's words. Who exactly will come, producing such amazing signs?

> say to those with fearful hearts,
> 'Be strong, do not fear;
> *your God will come,*
> he will come with vengeance;
> with divine retribution
> he will come to save you.'
> (Isaiah 35:4)

Could it be that John's disciples were hoping for those last three lines to come true – for God to take vengeance on his enemies (and save their master from Herod in the process)? Jesus, however, points to the very *next* verse – the signs that prove God has indeed arrived.

But wait! If Jesus is pointing to the things that *he himself* is doing, and then is quoting a scripture that promises that exactly those things would happen *when God comes*, then . . . who has come? Exactly what is Jesus saying? Nothing less than that, in his own coming, God himself has come.

Isaiah 35 is one of those massive prophetic passages that works on at least three levels, stretching to three horizons. And each horizon is a place of advent rejoicing!

First, it brought hope to the exiles of Judah. God was about to come and deliver them out of Babylon with a whole new exodus experience, described in effusive poetic imagery. He would lead them through the wilderness and provide for their needs (verses 1, 6b–7). They would be 'redeemed' by God (like Israel out of Egypt), and would return to Jerusalem with great rejoicing (verse 10).

The second horizon, of course, is the one Jesus himself pointed out to John's disciples – the gospel horizon of fulfilment: God came when Jesus came. That advent came with all the signs of the breaking in of the reign of God, and would finally lead to the cross and resurrection and ascension of the Messiah. We rejoice in the gospel!

And the third horizon still awaits us. For Isaiah's glorious vision points us forward to a totally transformed world, the renewal of all creation, the judgment and rectification of all wrongdoing, the end of all sickness and suffering, and the triumphant entry of God's redeemed people into the city of God, with everlasting joy that will banish all sorrow and tears. How about that for Advent rejoicing!

A prayer

We lift up before you, Heavenly Father, all those who are in prison today because of their faithful and courageous witness to your Son. Draw close to them by your Spirit in times when their faith is tested beyond anything we can imagine. Remind them of scriptures that confirm the truth of the gospel. Hold before their eyes the glorious hope of your coming, and grant that we, with them, may be faithful to the end, in the name of Jesus Christ our Lord. Amen.

20

Light for the nations

Bible reading: Luke 2:22–35

From John Stott:

> After I received Jesus Christ as my Saviour and Lord, one
> of the first ways in which I knew that something had
> happened to me was that the Bible became a new book . . .
> God began to speak to me; verses became luminous, phos-
> phorescent.
> (JS: TMOAL, p. 99)

> Simeon had the spiritual discernment to recognize Jesus . . .
> Firstly, Simeon saw Jesus as *the salvation of God*. What his
> eyes had actually seen was Mary's child; what he said he had
> seen was God's salvation, the Messiah God had sent to liberate
> us from the penalty and prison of sin.
>
> Secondly, Simeon saw Jesus as *the light of the world*, who
> would both enlighten the nations and bring glory to Israel
> (Isaiah 49:6). Thirdly, Simeon saw Jesus as *a cause of division*,
> a rock that some would stumble over and others would build
> on . . .
>
> Confronted by Jesus, neutrality is impossible. The story of
> Simeon is a lesson in spiritual recognition. May God give us
> the discernment to see beneath surface appearances to the
> reality of Jesus Christ!
> (TBTY, p. 155)

*

Simeon had only one item on his bucket list: 'See the Messiah.'[1] No catalogue of 'Fifty things to do before you die' for Simeon. Just this: 'See God's salvation. See God bringing comfort and hope to Israel and the world.'

For Luke, Simeon is a key witness among a whole cast of those who recognized the significance of the birth of Jesus in relation to Israel, and indeed the whole world. Luke's Gospel begins and ends with recognition of Jesus. In chapter 2 we meet the Temple Two (Simeon and Anna), longing for the consolation of Israel, and they recognize it in the baby Jesus. And in chapter 24 we meet the Emmaus Two (Cleopas and a friend, or his wife), longing for the redemption of Israel, and (eventually!) they recognized it in the risen Jesus.

The hope Simeon held in his heart (verses 25–26). Simeon is described, like Zechariah and Elizabeth, as a good Old Testament saint: righteous, devout, endowed with God's Spirit and with his eyes on God's future. His mind was filled with the Scriptures, longing for what Isaiah promised: 'Comfort, comfort my people.' Simeon wanted God to come and do that for Israel. He wanted God to reveal his glory for all the world to see (Isaiah 40:1–5). And Simeon knew (he had it in person from God) that he would indeed see God's salvation before he died, embodied in the person of *the Lord's Messiah.*

So here is Simeon, then, saturated with the Scriptures, believing the promises, alive to the Spirit, waiting for God. Advent hope embodied. An example to us all, wouldn't you say?

The child Simeon held in his arms (verses 27–30). It's a touching scene. Simeon is prompted to go into the temple courts, a crowded place. Quite possibly, there were other parents with babies shuffling around. But God's Spirit points out Mary and Joseph to Simeon and says, 'That's the one you're looking for.' Remember, Simeon is longing to *see God's salvation.* Gently, Simeon takes the baby from Mary's arms and, almost certainly (don't you think?), asks the baby's name. And Mary whispers, 'We've called him Yeshua, "The Lord's salvation".'

---

1 I owe this image to Stephen James, in a sermon preached on BBC Radio 4's *Sunday Worship.*

And Simeon breaks into his song of praise and thanks and wonder. 'Lord, this is to die for! Now I can die content. There's nothing worth living for more than this. My eyes have seen your salvation, your Yeshua, your anointed one, right here in my own arms.'

It is usually assumed, because he talks about dying, that Simeon was an old man, just waiting to 'depart'. Maybe he was, but Luke never actually mentions that he was old (whereas he does with Anna, verse 36). What if he was in the prime of life? How would you hear Simeon's words then? Nothing else in his life would ever surpass this moment. Holding Jesus, he could die right now and not regret it. That's how much it meant to him that God had kept his promise to his people.

But where are all these phrases coming from – 'peace', 'salvation', 'see with my own eyes', 'comfort', 'in the sight of all peoples'? Remember Isaiah 52:7–10? Please take another look at that wonderful passage. Can you hear the echoes and connections?

The prophet sings out the good news that God reigns, that God redeems (bringing peace, comfort, salvation, joy) and that God is returning. And here is God right now returning to his temple – as a baby! Advent in an infant. Simeon sees all that beautiful good news of Isaiah, wrapped up in the bundle in his arms, a tiny wee scrap of humanity called Jesus, the Creator and Saviour of the world.

So Luke wants us to see Jesus through Simeon's eyes. We need to see Christ's advent as the fulfilment of Israel's hopes, Israel's identity and Israel's mission. We recognize Jesus in the light of the Old Testament Scriptures. And, with Simeon, we rejoice!

The light Simeon holds out for the world (verses 31–32). Simeon didn't stop with what his own eyes had seen. The eyes of the whole world need to see what God has prepared for their salvation. Simeon knew well that the mission of Israel was to be the means of God's blessing to the rest of the nations, as God had promised Abraham (Genesis 12:3; Isaiah 42:6; 49:6). Simeon would have sung the Psalms daily, including words such as these, which are echoed in his own song:

The LORD has made his salvation known
  and revealed his righteousness to the nations.
He has remembered his love
  and his faithfulness to Israel;
all the ends of the earth have seen
  the salvation of our God.
(Psalm 98:2–3)

And so this little baby Jesus will be both 'a light for revelation to the Gentiles [nations], and the glory of your people Israel'.

Simeon does not explain how, but Luke does. Jesus instructs his disciples that 'repentance for the forgiveness of sins will be preached in his name to all nations, beginning at Jerusalem. You are witnesses of these things' (Luke 24:47–48).

And the Light of the World shines through the light of his witnesses, in the mission of the church (Acts 13:47; 26:23).

A challenge

Have we, with Simeon, recognized the authentic Scripture-fulfilling Jesus? Have we then not only embraced his identity, but also accepted his mission? We cannot hold him in our hearts unless we also hold him out to the world through the mission of witnessing to him among the nations.

21

The sin-bearing Servant

Bible reading: Isaiah 52:13 – 53:12

From John Stott:

> Christ died for us. Christ died instead of us (Romans 5:8) . . .
> neither Christ alone, nor God alone, but God in Christ.
> (IS, p. 217)

> Particularly the fifty-third chapter of Isaiah, describing the
> servant's suffering and death, is applied consistently to Jesus
> Christ . . . The New Testament writers quote eight specific
> verses as having been fulfilled in Jesus . . . Indeed, there is
> good evidence that his whole public career, from his baptism
> through his ministry, sufferings and death to his resurrection
> and ascension, is seen as a fulfilment of the pattern foretold in
> Isaiah 53.
> (TCOC, pp. 145–146)

*

I think it was a Roy Rogers Cowboy Annual that I got for this one.

When I was a child, my mother insisted that I learn whole
chapters of the Bible by heart. And when I could stand in front of
her and recite a chapter word perfect, I would get a reward that
I could choose for myself. And Isaiah 53 was one of the chapters
she prescribed for me to memorize. Its beautifully mysterious
phrases in the old KJV still surface when I call it to mind: 'a man
of sorrows and acquainted with grief . . . smitten of God and
afflicted . . . wounded for our transgressions . . . all we like sheep
have gone astray . . . the chastisement of our peace . . . with his

stripes we are healed . . . he shall see of the travail of his soul and be satisfied.'

What did it all mean? Well, I knew, as a very young believer, that in some sense it had to do with Jesus and his death and resurrection, and that was enough for me (and my mother) to allow the more puzzling phrases to remain wrapped in their enigmatic imagery.

Though I learned it beginning at 53:1, we need to go back to 52:13 for the real start of the passage (I don't blame my mother for not spotting that!). For this is a vision of the Servant of the Lord – a mysterious figure in these chapters. Please join me for a very quick tour.

Israel itself was called to be God's servant, to serve God's purpose in the world for the sake of the nations (remember Abraham? 41:8-10). But Israel was a failed and virtually disqualified servant, languishing in exile because of its sin and rebellion (42:18-25). So God announces an individual Servant who would come to fulfil God's mission (42:1-9). This Servant would be not only for Israel, but for all the ends of the earth as well (49:1-7). But he would suffer frustration, rejection and abuse (50:4-9) – and much worse (chapter 53). Nevertheless, God would accomplish his victorious purpose through this surprising – no, *shocking* – story.

It's a story in three parts.

God announces the plan (52:13-15). We learn the end of the story right at the start (which is reassuring). God foretells that he *will* exalt 'my servant' (verse 13). That is the big truth to keep in mind through all that follows. There will be a good ending! BUT, on the way to that glorious climax, God's Servant will go through the most appalling suffering, beyond human belief or imagination (verse 14).

'We' tell the story (53:1-11a). Unidentified speakers ('we') give a report about this Servant, now identified as 'the arm of the LORD' (52:10). First of all, we share honestly what we *originally* thought about him (verses 2-3). He was the kind of man that everybody despised, and we assumed that he was suffering under the just punishment of God for his own sin (verse 4b). So we rejected him, like everybody else.

But then, in a sudden and total reversal of our previous assessment, we now realize that he was suffering *for us* (verses 4–6). Everything he went through was in our place. God laid *our* sins on *him*. His death was a complete travesty of justice (verses 7–9). He was perfectly innocent, but he did not defend himself. So he was condemned to death and burial like a common criminal – yet somehow it was God's doing (verse 10a)!

But our story isn't finished. For even though he died, he will see his children! How can that be? Death will not be the end for the Servant of the Lord, for in some foreshadowing of the resurrection, he will be vindicated, he will see the light of life and will accomplish God's plan (verses 10b–11a).

God declares the outcome (53:11b–12). Now God takes over, and speaks about 'my righteous servant'. Because he bore the sins of many in his own death, he will enable many to be counted righteous by God. That will be the triumph of God's saving plan, and God will reward his Servant like the victor in a great battle.

It is impossible to read this astonishing chapter as a Christian without seeing in it a remarkable poetic and prophetic sketch of the life, death and resurrection of our Lord Jesus Christ. And it is clear, from many echoes of this chapter in the New Testament, that Jesus and his disciples understood it that way.

How do you think we should respond?

Remember, first of all, that every aspect of the coming of Jesus was in accordance with the promises of the Old Testament Scriptures (what this week's readings have been about). Be very clear, today, that the cross of Jesus was also entirely part of God's plan. It was not some kind of ghastly accident that had to be put right by the resurrection. It was, as Peter said on the day of Pentecost, part of God's will and purpose from the beginning, even though it was carried out by wicked people with full responsibility for their actions (Acts 2:22–24). As Paul puts it, Jesus died for our sins and rose again *'according to the Scriptures'* (1 Corinthians 15:3–4) – scriptures such as this one.

And second, we need to see ourselves among the 'we/us' of Isaiah 53. This is the language of *testimony*, and it is both negative ('we despised him') and the reverse – gloriously positive ('it was for us'). Part of our repentance can be to ask whether there are ways in which we have treated Jesus with contempt. But, equally, part of our rejoicing should be the deep-down realization of verses 4–6. It was for me!

Bearing shame and scoffing rude
in my place condemned he stood
sealed my pardon with his blood.
Hallelujah! What a Saviour![1]

An exercise

The pattern of the Servant is the pattern for us also. Suffering is part of Christian experience, and our response should reflect the way of Christ. Read these words of Peter (1 Peter 2:20–25; 3:13–18; 4:12–19). Can you see how much he has absorbed from Isaiah 53? I dare say Peter's mother made him memorize that chapter too, before he ever met Jesus.

---

1   P. P. Bliss, 'Man of Sorrows, What a Name', 1875.

Week 4

THE GOD WHO WILL COME IN GLORY

We began our journey by seeing how the great theme of *the God who comes* is woven through every act of the drama of Scripture. God keeps on coming, as the story moves forward through history. And then we focused on the greatest single moment of God's coming prior to the Lord Jesus Christ – the exodus. We explored several ways in which the book of Exodus shows God coming, and for different reasons and outcomes. In our third week, we saw how Jesus came 'in accordance with the Scriptures' – that is, as the climax of a whole trajectory of promises built into the story so far. So, in these final days in Christmas week itself, we follow the dynamic of Advent right through to its grand climax.

For the One who came as God in a manger in Bethlehem is the One who will come again, to complete God's great plan of redemption for the whole universe. We rejoice that he came, that he was born to die once for all, for us and for our salvation. We rejoice even more that he will come once more, to reign with us for ever, in his creation renewed, redeemed and reconciled through the blood of his cross.

A prayer for week 4 of Advent

Heavenly Father, who chose the virgin Mary, full of grace, to be the mother of our Lord and Saviour, fill us with your grace, that in all things we may accept your holy will and with her rejoice in your salvation, through Jesus Christ our Lord. Amen.

22

Creation rejoices

Bible reading: Psalm 96

John Stott really welcomed the lively, upbeat music of these new rhythmic congregational songs . . . 'All Souls (Church) music has enlivened my soul no end,' he once told me. (Noel Tredennick, JS: APBHF, pp. 180, 183)

He is already King, but the earth does not yet acknowledge His rule. So He is coming to judge the earth, and its peoples.

Only when God's rule is established on earth (. . . begun . . . through Christ . . .), will the peoples and nature itself be subdued and righteously governed. He who has already shown His righteousness in the saving of His people, will exhibit it again in His judging of the world. This judgment will include the punishment of the wicked, as is made plain in Isaiah 11:1–5. But . . . we shall recognize that 'true and just are his judgments', and concurring with them we shall cry, 'Amen, Hallelujah!' (Revelation 19:1–5).
(John Stott, FP, p. 90)

*

I wonder what the Israelites thought when one of their songwriters began, 'Sing to the LORD a new song'? Especially when he launched into it and it was full of all the old words. A new song, he says, but it's all about God's *name*, God's *salvation*, God's *glory* and God's *marvellous deeds* (verses 1–3)! Those are the old songs we've been singing since Moses brought us up out of Egypt! Is this a remix, a cover song, or what? What's new about it?

What's new is not the words themselves, but where the song is going to be sung: in *all the earth, among the nations*, and *among all peoples*. An old song for Israel (celebrating the name and salvation and glory of their God Yahweh) will become a new song by new singers to the ends of the earth, as they come to know the living God for themselves. This is a missional song that looks to the future, God's future, a new song that *refreshes the old words*, as they become the salvation songs of the nations in all the earth.

This is also a new song that *displaces the old gods* (verses 4–9). For it looks to the future when people of all nations will recognize how empty and futile are the gods they worship (and we have plenty of idols in the West too, even if we don't think of them in religious language). Instead, the song invites the whole world to bring their worship into the presence of the only true and living God, to worship *him* in the beauty of *his* holiness. Mission means singing the song of our Saviour God, and inviting the nations to join the choir.

And at its climax, this is a new song that *transforms the old world* (verses 10–13). The psalmist calls on Israel to proclaim that Yahweh their God is King (verse 10) – but not just over Israel. No, the kingdom of God is over all nations and the whole world (you're still remembering Abraham, I hope!).

The song 'undescribes' the world as we know it today, and calls on our imagination to envisage the world as it will be when God comes to reign. This is advent hope in the imagination of poetry and song!

So what will it be like when God reigns over all the earth? It will be a world of reliability – stable and 'firmly established' – as it was at creation (verse 10). The world we know (in the psalmist's day, as much as our own) is a world of chaotic instability, among the nations and in the physical world of nature and climate. But not for ever. God's reign will restore the world order that God decrees, and we shall be secure.

It will be a world of righteousness and fairness ('equity', verses 10b and 13b). The world the psalmist knew, like our world, was bulging and collapsing under the weight of injustice, oppression and cruelty. But not for ever. When God comes to reign, he will put all things right, which is what verse 13 means:

He will judge the world in righteousness
    and the peoples in his faithfulness.

And above all, it will be a world of rejoicing. *Rejoice!* (our book title) echoes the call of the psalm. But, let's face it, the world we know is filled with incalculable grief, mourning and tears, not only from the mountain of human suffering, but also from the groaning of creation itself under the devastation of human wickedness and wastefulness. I sometimes wonder, when my own heart is broken and my eyes in tears at the sight of yet more starving and homeless and brutalized children – how can God bear it? God who sees the pain of every child on earth, and every grieving parent, and every life shattered by weapons and maiming, not to mention every dying animal species, every poisoned, hunted and tangled creature, and every piece of polluted land and sea and air?

But not for ever! The climax of our new song explodes in an anthem of whole-creation rejoicing, like a great *Ode to Joy*. When God comes to reign, all creation will rejoice. The poetry soars, as we imagine the sea resounding, the fields rejoicing, the trees singing, the rivers clapping their hands and the mountains singing together (Psalm 98:8). Poetic metaphors, but also profound truth.

Let all creation rejoice before the Lord, *for he comes.* That is the joy of Advent, which Paul says we share with creation itself (Romans 8:18–21). This week we look forward to Christmas. Let us also join all creation in looking forward to the day when Psalm 96 comes true.

Here is how William Cowper imagines it:

Rivers of gladness water all the earth,
And clothe all climes with beauty. The reproach
Of barrenness is past. The fruitful field
Laughs with abundance; and the land, once lean
Or fertile only in its own disgrace,
Exults to see its thistly curse repeal'd . . .

One song employs all nations; and all cry,
'Worthy the Lamb, for He was slain for us!'
The dwellers in the vales and on the rocks
Shout to each other, and the mountain tops
From distant mountains catch the flying joy;
Till, nation after nation taught the strain,
Earth rolls the rapturous Hosanna round.[1]

---

1   Excerpt from 'The Task', 1785.

23

Creation renewed

Bible readings: Isaiah 65:17–25; 2 Peter 3:3–13

From John Stott:

> We are caught in the painful tension between the 'now' and the 'not yet'.
> (TW, TCC series, p. 92)

Have Christians a distinctive contribution to make to the ecological debate? Yes, we believe both that God created the earth, entrusting its care to us, and that he will one day recreate it, when he makes 'the new heavens and the new earth' . . . These two doctrines, regarding the beginning and the end of history, the creation and the consummation, have a profound effect on our perspective. They give us appropriate respect for the earth, indeed for the whole material creation, since God both made it and will remake it.

In consequence, we must learn to think and act ecologically. We repent of extravagance, pollution and wanton destruction. We recognize that human beings find it easier to subdue the earth than they do to subdue themselves.
(IFCT, p. 155)

*

Have you seen what amazing things expert restorers can do with old paintings these days? They can take an oil painting that has become blackened and encrusted with centuries of dust, grease, candle smoke and human carelessness, and, with great care and powerful substances, restore it to what it looked like when it left the artist's hands. It can seem like a totally new work of art, and yet in fact it is the original, restored to its intended beauty and glory.

They can do the same astonishingly transformative work of restoration on worn-out antique furniture, and even rusting and cannibalized old railway steam engines. Things old and spoiled and broken can be made as good as new – the same original artefact, yet salvaged and renewed, released (redeemed, we might say) from the accumulated dirt and damage of the years.

If human beings are capable of doing that with things we ourselves have made, how much more is the Creator of the universe capable of doing it with the work of his hands? For indeed, in the Bible God tells us that that is exactly what he plans to do. 'See, I will create new heavens and a new earth,' he says, using the same Hebrew word as in Genesis 1 for the unique creative work of God (Isaiah 65:17). But as the prophet describes what God means, he clearly is not thinking of some totally different place 'up in heaven', but rather the fullness and joy of life on earth – this earth restored to health, life, fruitfulness and harmony, renewed and purged of all the filthy effects of sin and evil.

Won't it be amazing to live happily, with no more tears (verse 19), in a world where death, especially infant death, is banished (verse 20; the language is rhetorical)? Won't it be wonderful to have a fulfilling family life, in which your home and the fruit of your hard work could never be stolen by injustice (verses 21–22)? What wouldn't you give to prevent your children and grandchildren suffering (verse 23)? Imagine if God were so close that his blessing didn't even need to be asked for (verse 24)? Imagine if the whole world of nature were freed from destruction and harm (verse 25)?

'Wait for it,' says God. 'That's just a tiny snapshot. You can't imagine all that I will bring about in the new creation that I am already working on.' That's what Paul has in mind when he tells us that God's ultimate mission is to heal and unify the whole universe under Christ (Ephesians 1:9–10), and indeed he has reconciled all creation to himself through the blood of Christ shed on the cross (Colossians 1:15–20). That's what feeds John's vision of the coming new creation – the final wonderful advent in the whole drama of Scripture (Revelation 21 – 22).

Rejoice! That's what God is preparing for us! Creation renewed and restored.

But wait a minute, we might respond. Doesn't Peter tell us that the whole universe will end up in some cosmic incinerator? People who think that is what Peter means in 2 Peter 3 sometimes oppose Christians getting involved in environmental issues, by saying, 'If creation is all going to be burnt up, why should we care for it now?' But even if it were true, is that a sensible question to ask?

Suppose you go to the doctor with serious pains in your body, and she says, 'Well, you're going to die anyway, and your body will end up in a crematorium, so why should I care for it now?' You'd get out of her surgery pretty fast. The body is God's good creation gift, so we care for human bodies, and, as Christians, we believe in the resurrection of the body – no matter what happens to it at death. The same is true of creation (and Paul makes precisely that connection, as we will see tomorrow).

But is that what Peter actually meant? Look at the balance of the chapter. Peter is dealing with people who were mocking the whole idea of advent. There will be no 'coming' of God in judgment, they sneer (verses 3–4). But they forget that God *did* once judge the earth, in the waters of the flood, by which the world was 'destroyed' (verses 5–6). And in the same way, God *will* judge the earth, but this time by fire (verse 7). So the language of fiery conflagration and destruction that follows signifies *purging and cleansing* of the earth from all sin and evil ('destruction of the ungodly', verse 7) – not total obliteration, any more than the earth itself was 'destroyed' in the flood. God will obliterate evil, not obliterate creation.

So, as we saw on day 6 of week 1, Advent reminds us that there certainly will be a final day of judgment, and it will bring about the judgment of all unrepentant evildoers and the final eradication of all evil from God's universe. And that is what Peter means by his apocalyptic imagery of *that day*.

And after that? Well, Peter tells us what is coming next, with a clear reference to God's promise in Isaiah 65. 'In keeping with his promise we are looking forward to a new heaven and a new earth, where righteousness dwells' (verse 13). Bible drama act 7 kicks in after act 6 (see diagram on p. 2). First, God will put all things right, and then he will make all things new. No wonder creation itself eagerly longs for its renewal. So do we. That's one big part of what Advent is all about, something we can rejoice about, along with creation itself.

Living in the light of the new creation: a challenge

So then, dear friends, since you are looking forward to this, make every effort to be found spotless, blameless and at peace with him ... grow in the grace and knowledge of our Lord and Saviour Jesus Christ. To him be glory both now and for ever! Amen.
(2 Peter 3:14, 18)

24

Creation redeemed

Bible reading: Romans 8:16–25

From John Stott:

> Paul likened nature's frustration, bondage to decay and groans to 'the pains of childbirth' . . . references to the promise of cosmic renewal for both society and nature . . . not applied in the Bible to the salvation of individuals or people.
> (TCOC, p. 375)

We must hold on to Paul's combination of present sufferings and future glory. Each verse expresses it. The creation's subjection to frustration was in hope (20). The bondage to decay will give place to the freedom of glory (21). The pains of labour will be followed by the joys of birth (22). There is therefore going to be both continuity and discontinuity in the regeneration of the world, as in the resurrection of the body. The universe is not going to be destroyed, but rather liberated, transformed and suffused with the glory of God.
(BST, *Romans*, p. 241)

*

'Don't put it there! Your son's in that cot!' cried the midwife.

I had arrived in the bedroom with a tray laden with a pot of tea and mugs and was about to place it on the little Moses basket awaiting, as I thought, our yet-to-be-born baby. It was a home birth and I was doing my husbandly best. But as my wife's contractions reached their apparent climax, the midwife sent me downstairs to make tea, and by the time I came back, the wee chap had already arrived and been wrapped and laid in his cot while the midwife did the needful for Liz.

The miracle of birth gets no less special just because it happens every few seconds around the world. So I love how Paul chooses that as a way of picturing the arrival of the new creation.

It's as if, he says, this old creation is groaning (as we know and see only too well all around us), *but* it is groaning with the pangs of childbirth. The new creation is already being brought to birth within the womb of this creation. So creation's pain and frustration are embraced within the hope and joy of the birth and new life that lie ahead.

This is a wonderful metaphor, which suggests three things to me.

First, as John Stott says above, there is discontinuity within continuity. Birth is a definitive moment in anybody's life (to say the least). You are no longer a foetus in the womb, but breathing air in the outside world. Life is totally different now, and yet in so many ways you are of course the same person as that baby in the womb. All that you physically are now and will become has its origin and structure already formed. And birth is irreversible; you can't go back (as puzzled Nicodemus pointed out).

The new creation will not simply be this old creation scrubbed up a bit. Nor will it be a completely other and different creation altogether. There will be a transformation as radical and dynamic and spectacular as from the foetus to the breathing, seeing, crying, responding post-natal human life, with all its potential. Something unimaginable from the perspective of the womb, and yet the same human being. The new creation will be recognizably *this creation* – in which we will know ourselves to be at home, know that this is what creation was destined for. And there'll be no going back to how things were before.

Second, there is no way a foetus in the womb can begin to imagine what life will be like outside the womb – *even though it has all the potential equipment in its brain and sensory systems to live that new life when the time comes.*

'Do you believe all this stuff about "life after birth" then?' says one baby in the womb to its twin (let's suppose). 'All these rumours we hear about "light" and "air" and "colour" and "breathing" and "walking" and all?'

'No, no,' replies the twin. 'That's all just a myth to help us cope with this place. No, there's nothing else "out there". Amniotic fluid – that's all there is. When you're born, you're born – that's it, finished, all over. The End.'

Living in the womb of this creation, we cannot conceive (pun unintended) of whole new dimensions of resurrection life in the new creation, any more than a foetus can conceive of the wonders of life in the new world it is destined for. Yet it is coming! Unstoppably coming! Every birth is an advent. The end of life in the womb is the beginning of life in God's world.

When I preach or teach about the new creation, I sometimes get asked questions like, 'How's that all going to happen, then?' 'What's it going to be like when we get there?' 'What age will we be?' And I have to say, I simply don't know. All we *do* know are the pictures and analogies that God gives us in the Bible, which tell us that it will be gloriously fulfilling and better than the very best we can enjoy or even imagine in this world and this life. Just because we can't imagine *how* it will all happen doesn't mean we don't believe *that* it will be as God promised.

And third, Paul links the birth of the new creation to the redemption of our bodies. 'The creation waits in eager expectation for the children of God to be revealed', and meanwhile 'we wait eagerly for our adoption to sonship, the redemption of our bodies' (verses 19, 23). Every birth is, in a sense, a liberation of the 'captive' baby in the womb into the glorious freedom of life in this world. So it will be when the Lord returns and we receive our resurrection bodies, like Christ's (1 Corinthians 15:51–53; Philippians 3:21; 1 John 3:2). At that moment, creation too will be liberated from its bondage (verse 21).

Liberation! Redemption! Those are Advent words for us, for all lands, all peoples, and for all creation.

I wonder if you are looking forward to that day as eagerly as creation itself is, according to Paul? For we are not going to be saved *out of* the earth, but we shall be saved *along with* the earth. That is the unimaginable but clearly revealed cosmic plan of God for the reconciliation of heaven and earth and all creation. And it has been accomplished through the shed blood of Christ on the cross (Colossians 1:20), the One whose birth we will celebrate tomorrow.

> *I cannot tell* how all the lands shall worship,
> when, at his bidding, every storm is stilled,
> or who can say how great the jubilation
> when every heart with love and joy is filled.
> *But this I know,* the skies will thrill with rapture,
> and myriad, myriad human voices sing,
> and earth to heav'n, and heav'n to earth, will answer,
> 'At last the Saviour, Saviour of the world, is King!'[1]

---

1 William Y. Fullerton, 'I Cannot Tell', 1920.

25

Immanuel: God with us!

Bible reading: Revelation 21:1–5

From John Stott:

> I have a living hope of a yet more glorious life beyond
> death . . .
> (Quoted by Chris Wright, funeral sermon, 2011)

One day the Jesus who died, rose and reigns will return. He
who is hidden will appear. His second coming, moreover, will
be quite different from his first . . . He who came in humility
and shame will return in spectacular magnificence . . . And
when he appears, we shall appear 'with him'. Our secret will
be out. Our identity will be disclosed. Our hidden life will be
made manifest. We shall be known for who we are, by God's
sheer mercy his redeemed children. We shall see – and in
some sense beyond our comprehending – share his glory.
(LIC, p. 69)

*

Veiled in flesh, the Godhead see;
Hail, th'incarnate Deity:
Pleased, as man, with man to dwell,
Jesus, our Emmanuel.
(Charles Wesley, 'Hark! the Herald Angels Sing', 1739)

You may well sing those words today, and you may already
have sung Charles Wesley's rich and resonant Christmas hymn,
'Hark! the Herald Angels Sing' in the last week or two. *Jesus, our*

Emmanuel. Jesus, our 'With-us God'. The God who *came* for that very purpose: to be with us, to take our humanity into himself, and then in our human flesh to bear the consequences of our sin.

And, connecting with yesterday's reflection, the marvel is that Christ's first advent was to come into the world the way we all do, through the ovary, fallopian tube, womb and birth canal of a woman.

> God of God, light of light,
> Lo, he abhors not the Virgin's womb.

I am amazed every Christmas at this miracle of incarnation: the Creator of the universe, by the power of his Holy Spirit, became a single fertilized ovum, a minuscule zygote cell of human tissue. God did not just *arrive* as some extra-terrestrial superhero. God was *born* into his own creation. Advent in pain and blood and joy and a manger.

> 'Twas much, that man was made like God before,
> But, that God should be made like man, much more.[1]

'O come, O come, Emmanuel . . .' we also sing through Advent, with a minor key tune that somehow never quite seems to match the summons of the refrain, 'Rejoice! Rejoice! Emmanuel / shall come to thee, O Israel.' Of course, we sing it from the perspective of Old Testament Israel, longing for the coming of their Messiah. But we sing it also with our longing for his coming again. It is a double-duty Advent hymn.

There is, of course, a vast contrast between Christ's first coming and his second. He came in humility, seen and recognized as Messiah by only a few; he will return in glory, seen by every eye and acknowledged as Lord by every knee and tongue on the planet.

Our reading today opens our eyes, with John's, to that glorious day. The profuse imagery of his language tumbles over itself to

---

1 John Donne, *Holy Sonnets*, XV, 1896.

express the transformation. No more 'sea' (meaning the chaotic evil that 'the sea' represents in the Bible). No more death, or mourning. No more darkness, no more sin, no more curse (21:22 – 22:5). A new creation in which *the old order of things has passed away.*

Rejoice!

Rejoice too, today, in one thing that the first and second advents have in common. The clue is in the word: 'advent'. It was, and will be, *God coming.* It means God doing what God does all through Scripture, as we have seen. God comes to be with us; God does not whisk us off at the end to be with him somewhere else. There's a reason why we call it the season of Advent, not the season of Exit. The climax of the whole drama of Scripture, the last great vision of the whole Bible, is *God coming,* not *us going.*

We link the name *Immanuel* very readily with Christmas. The Baby of Bethlehem is manifestly God with us. 'The Word became flesh and made his dwelling among us' (John 1:14). But did you also notice the triple echo of Immanuel in Revelation 21:3? Three times it comes: 'the dwelling place of God is *with man.* He will dwell *with them* . . . and God himself will be *with them* as their God' (ESV). God comes to be with us, intimately and for ever. Advent is the ultimate realization of Immanuel. Here comes the 'With-us God'.

It is still a common idea that our final destiny is to 'go up to heaven'. Even that most popular of all Christian hymns, 'How Great Thou Art', envisages, 'When Christ shall come, with shout of acclamation, and take me home . . .' No! He comes to *make his home* – here with us, his redeemed people, in his restored creation, not to take us to some other home than the one he created for us and redeemed through the blood of his Son.

Now, of course, those who die in Christ do indeed go to be with him, safe and secure in the meantime until he returns and we are clothed with resurrection bodies. But the Bible does not end with us going up, but with *God coming down,* with the arrival of the new heaven and new earth, the city of God. Rejoice today in that great prospect, guaranteed by the One who first came down to make it possible.

So let's finish our Advent journey of rejoicing with another great hymn of Charles Wesley, with which I have only one disagreement in its final Advent-focused verse.

Rejoice, the Lord is King!
Your Lord and King adore;
Rejoice, give thanks and sing,
And triumph evermore;
Lift up your heart, lift up your voice;
Rejoice, again I say, rejoice!

Jesus, the Saviour, reigns,
The God of truth and love;
When He had purged our stains
He took His seat above;
Lift up your heart, lift up your voice;
Rejoice, again I say, rejoice!

His kingdom cannot fail,
He rules o'er earth and Heav'n,
The keys of death and hell
Are to our Jesus giv'n;
Lift up your heart, lift up your voice;
Rejoice, again I say, rejoice!

Rejoice in glorious hope!
Jesus the Judge shall come,
And take His servants up
To their eternal home;
We soon shall hear th' archangel's voice;
The trump of God shall sound, rejoice!

The only thing that 'goes up' will be the joy and praise of the unified creation of the new heaven and earth and all the redeemed who will dwell there. We will already be 'home', with God dwelling in our midst. It will once again be his home and ours.

So Jesus is not coming to take us somewhere else, but to make his eternal home here with us – that's what the Bible says.

I wonder if Charles Wesley would allow a slight change of two lines . . .

Rejoice in glorious hope!
Jesus the Judge shall come,
Creation's joy goes up
From God's eternal home.
We soon shall hear th' archangel's voice:
The trump of God shall sound, rejoice!